It's Your Attitude

It's Your **Attitude**

Out with the Bad, In with the Good

Chris Thurman

CASCADE *Books* • Eugene, Oregon

IT'S YOUR ATTITUDE
Out with the Bad, In with the Good

Cascade Books
An Imprint of Wipf and Stock Publishers
199 W. 8th Ave., Suite 3
Eugene, OR 97401

www.wipfandstock.com

PAPERBACK ISBN: 978-1-7252-8160-8
HARDCOVER ISBN: 978-1-7252-8159-2
EBOOK ISBN: 978-1-7252-8161-5

Cataloguing-in-Publication data:

Names: Thurman, Chris, author.

Title: It's Your Attitude : Out with the bad, in with the good / by Chris Thurman.

Description: Eugene, OR: Cascade Books, 2021.

Identifiers: ISBN 978-1-7252-8160-8 (paperback) | ISBN 978-1-7252-8159-2 (hardcover) | ISBN 978-1-7252-8161-5 (ebook)

Subjects: LCSH: Maturation (Psychology). | Interpersonal relations. | Spirituality. | Common fallacies.

Classification: BF638 .T50 2021 (print) | BF638 (ebook)

06/01/21

Attitude is a little thing that makes a big difference.

—Winston Churchill

Contents

How to Have a Good Attitude for Life

Introduction

There's an old (and corny) joke we psychologists often tell. "How many psychologists does it take to change a lightbulb? One, but it really has to want to change."

In light of the focus of this book, I want to rewrite that joke and ask, "How many people does it take to change a bad attitude? One, but you really have to want to change." When it comes to changing the unhealthy attitude we have about life, liberty, and the pursuit of happiness, we have to give it our best effort. Anything less simply won't do.

The good news is that we can change our attitude for the better and experience a richer and fuller life as a result. It's not easy, but it's doable. The fact that we can change our attitude is the reason none of us need to despair or feel hopeless about how our lives turn out. I'm not promising you the sun, moon, and stars here, but, if you'll work on improving your attitude, you can make life just about as meaningful and enjoyable as you want it to be.

I have four main objectives in this book.

First, I'm going to explore the importance of a healthy attitude in determining how your brief time on this planet goes.

Second, I'm going to walk you through the twelve worst attitudes you can have as a human being, the toxic ones that are making your life miserable and blocking you from experiencing the life you want.

Third, I'm going to take you into the twelve best attitudes available, the transformational ones that can set you on a path to living life more fully.

Finally, I'm going to close the book by challenging you to spend the rest of your life working on improving your attitude. I'm going to do that so that when your time draws to a close you can look at yourself in the mirror and God in the face and know you did the best you could to live life well.

We only get one shot at life. We need to make sure we don't blow it by allowing toxic attitudes to make us and everyone around us miserable. We really do have the freedom to choose our attitude, and we need to use that freedom wisely. Life is much too short to allow unhealthy attitudes to ruin our journey through all the good and bad things that inevitably come our way.

So, how many people does it take to change a bad attitude? One, but you really have to want to change. Do you? Do you really want to overcome a bad attitude and develop a good one? If so, keep reading.

The Importance of
Changing Your Attitude

Chapter 1

We All Need a Major Attitude Adjustment

The most significant change in a person's life is a change of attitude.

—William J. Johnston

Finally, brothers and sisters, whatever is true, whatever is noble, whatever is right, whatever is pure, whatever is lovely, whatever is admirable—if anything is excellent or praiseworthy—think about such things.

—Philippians 4:8

Imagine a time in human history when you were ripped from your home because of your religious beliefs, shoehorned into trains like cattle, taken hundreds of miles away from all you were familiar with, stripped of everything you owned, separated from family members, forced to undress, subjected to your head being shaved and an identification number put on your arm, and housed in barracks that were so overcrowded that you had to sleep on your side and share one blanket with three or four other people.

Further imagine that the barracks you were housed in were so poorly constructed that rain leaked through the roof and made everything damp and moldy. The mattress you slept on was filthy, lice and rats were a major problem, the heater in the barracks wasn't sufficient for warming the whole room, and contagious diseases frequently erupted.

The barracks you lived in had no sinks or toilets, both of which were outside in unscreened "privies." To use them you had to undress and leave the barracks regardless of the weather. Because of the ratio of prisoners to sinks and toilets, you were lucky if you were able to use them at all. The water you washed in was dirty, there was no soap, and there was no change of clothes for weeks and even months at a time.

You were awakened early for roll call and had to stand at attention, oftentimes for hours, to be counted. Prisoners who died during the night were required to be included in the roll call and had to be brought out by those who had survived. You were fed three times a day but it was always a meager ration of watery soup, imitation coffee, a small piece of bread, and, on occasion, a wafer-thin slice of sausage. Mass starvation was common and those who didn't die from malnutrition were called "living skeletons."

Work, mirroring the living conditions, was inhumane. The typical work day was ten to twelve hours long, the gloves and coats provided were insufficient, you had to work with your hands if they didn't provide tools, the tools they gave you were inadequate, the work itself was often useless (moving dirt or rocks from one place to another for no reason), and you had to work fast or you were insulted, beaten, and even killed. You couldn't stop working and if you fainted you were beaten up or executed.

Can you imagine? I can't. Nothing I've experienced in my life allows me to imagine the horror of being in a situation so evil and inhumane as to make survival nearly impossible. Yet, some survived. Some who were not directly put to death or died from malnutrition, exhaustion, or disease actually made it through this horrible experience.

One of the survivors of the Nazi death camps was Austrian psychiatrist Viktor Frankl. He was interned in four concentration camps and lost his wife, mother, father, and brother to them. In spite of this horrific experience, Frankl not only survived but went on to write about his experiences in a book, *Man's Search for Meaning*. As an outgrowth of his experiences, Frankl developed an approach to psychotherapy that emphasized the search for purpose and meaning as the best way to cope with suffering and trauma. One of the conclusions he reached as a result of his concentration camp experiences is one of the most often quoted statements on the importance of attitude in life:

> We who lived in concentration camps can remember the men who walked through the huts comforting others, giving away their last piece of bread. They may have been few in number, but they offer sufficient proof that everything can be taken from a man but one thing: the last of the human freedoms—*to choose one's attitude in any given set of circumstances*, to choose one's own way.

The main takeaway from Frankl's quote is obvious—we have the freedom to choose our attitude regardless of the circumstances we are in, and, consequently, to choose our path through life. Everything was taken from those who suffered in Nazi concentration camps but this one thing—their attitude. If they could find purpose and meaning in their suffering, even if it was simply to stay alive so they could be reunited with loved ones, that could help them make it if disease, exhaustion, malnutrition, or execution didn't kill them.

It's painful to admit, but I don't think I would have been one of the few in number "who walked through the huts comforting others, giving away their last piece of bread." Had I been in a concentration camp, my attitude would probably not have been up to the test, and my feelings and actions would have mirrored that fact. I often find that my attitude isn't even up to the test when I run into the *minor hassles* of life, like someone riding my bumper in traffic, not finding what I need at the store, or having to wait in long lines. All the things that happen in life, from the minor irritations to the major traumas, test us and reveal to us whether or not we have the kind of attitude that will help us thrive or the kind of attitude that will cause our demise.

A Little Side Trip

That being said, let me take a little side trip. I want to suggest that there are four things that play a major role in how our lives turn out. First, there is the *nature* part of life, the physical body, genetics, and biology we come with that significantly impact how we function. Second, there is the *nurture* part of life, how people treat us along the way, which powerfully shapes how we feel about ourselves, others, life, and God. Third, there is the *nonphysical* realm of life, spiritual forces behind the scenes that nudge us in the direction of doing good or evil. Finally, there is the *attitude* part of life, how we choose to view the things that happen to us. Collectively, these are the four big-ticket items when it comes how our earthly life turns out.

We can't do much, if anything, about nature, nurture, and the nonphysical. We don't get to decide what kind of genetics/wiring/biology we are born with, how we are treated growing up, and what spiritual forces of good and evil are doing behind the scenes to duke it out over us. We can do a great deal to *steward* these three by taking good care of our body, healing from relational wounds that left us feeling worthless and unlovable, and yielding to *benevolent* spiritual forces that are out to help us grow into more mature and loving people. On top of all that, the biggest favor we can do ourselves is to work on improving our attitude.

William James, considered the father of American psychology, said, "The greatest revolution of our generation is the discovery that human beings, by changing the inner attitudes of their minds, can change the outer aspects of their lives." That's wise counsel we can base our lives on.

Whether we acknowledge it or not, we are responsible for the attitude we carry into each day. Because we have free will, we can either be our own worst enemy or our own best friend, depending on which attitudes we accept and which ones we reject. So, while we don't have a whole lot of say so about nature, nurture, and spiritual reality, we have a tremendous amount to say about what kind of attitude we take into our day-to-day lives.

Self-Help Psychology's Bad Attitude About Attitude

Even though I'm a psychologist, I have to tell you there are more than a few things I don't like about some of what comes out of pop psychology self-help books. When it comes to the issue of attitude, I find three pop psychology notions to be the most bothersome.

First, the idea that "attitude is everything." That's nonsense. As I mentioned earlier, the physical body we are born with, the way we are treated growing up, and spiritual forces of good and evil are not to be underestimated for how our earthly life turns out. I wouldn't be writing this book if our attitude in life wasn't a crucial issue, but, please, don't buy into the notion that attitude is *everything* and that if you just work on that one thing, you'll be fine. You could work on improving your attitude the rest of your life and still be fighting an uphill battle against nature, nurture, and spiritual forces of darkness.

Second, the idea "your attitude determines your altitude." That's nonsense as well. Some people would have achieved a much higher level of success in life if it weren't for the *downside* of nature, nurture, and the nonphysical. So many people would have soared to much greater heights if these three factors hadn't been working against them. So, don't guilt-trip yourself if you didn't reach the highest altitude you could have in life—it may not have had a whole lot to do with your attitude. There are a lot of factors out of our control that impact how high we soar in life. At the same time, don't make excuses if you didn't reach your full potential because you were lazy or made a lot of bad choices along the way. Far too many people cop out by blaming nature, nurture, and spiritual reality for how badly their lives turned out when it was primarily their own fault.

Third, the idea "you need to have a positive attitude." Again, this is misguided. The self-help authors and motivational speakers who promote positive thinking are not doing us any favors. In fact, they're causing us harm. The issue in life is not having a *positive* attitude but an *accurate* one. Some accurate ways of looking at things are negative. For example, there is evil in the world. That is accurate but a negative thing about life. On the other side of the coin, some accurate ways of looking at things are positive. For example, you are a fearfully and wonderfully made human being created in the image of God. Please, don't worry about whether your attitude is positive or negative—just focus on making sure it's accurate.

What I'm saying here is that I think some people in the self-help movement have a bad attitude about attitude. I could be dead wrong on this, but I would encourage you to see that attitude is important but not everything. Things other than your attitude have a significant impact on how your life turns out, and a positive attitude isn't near as important as an accurate one. Thank you for listening—I will now get down off my soap box.

Beliefs, Values, and Attitudes 101

Even among the experts, there is some confusion as to how beliefs, values, and attitudes differ from each other. I read as much as I could on this topic before my head began to explode and I became more confused. So, let me give you the best take I can on this issue while acknowledging that not every mental health professional would agree.

Beliefs are what you hold to be true whether you have evidence to back them up or not. For example, you might believe Hondas are better cars than Hyundais even if you don't have definitive evidence to support your belief. On the flip side, you may believe Hyundais are better cars than Hondas even though you don't have any definitive evidence to back that up either. The beliefs you have are shaped by experience, culture, faith, mentors, role models, education, and 400 other things.

Values are the things that are important to you. In today's world, people tend to value shallow things like wealth, happiness, success, and appearance. But our values can also include deeper things like honesty, hard work, responsibility, justice, decency, and integrity. Your beliefs pave the way to the values you hold.

Attitudes are comprised of three things: the beliefs you hold that reflect what you think is true, the values you have about what is important, and the way you act in light of what you think is important.

To drive this home, let's go back to the issue of Hondas versus Hyundais. Whichever car you prefer, you believe it to be the better car, place a higher value on owning one over your other options, and, when it comes time to plunk down your hard-earned money, you buy one car and not the other. In buying that particular brand of car, you are expressing your attitude that it was the wisest and best route to go.

The main takeaway here is that beliefs are what you hold to be true, values are what you hold to be important, and attitudes are a combination of beliefs and values that compel you to act a certain way. From my perspective, each of the bad attitudes we are about to explore are in the "bad" category because they reflect a tendency to believe something that isn't true and value something that isn't valuable. Conversely, each of the good attitudes we are going to examine reflect believing something that is true and valuing something that is important.

Some Final Thoughts

I think it's safe to say that most people in the mental health field will tell you that your attitude is *extremely* important. This is a widely accepted truth that cuts across numerous "people-helping" areas of life, religion included. Pastor Charles Swindoll expressed it this way:

> The longer I live the more convinced I am that life is 10 percent what happens to us and 90 percent how we respond to it. . . .
>
> I believe the single most significant decision I can make on a day-to-day basis is my choice of attitude. It is more important than my past, my education, my bankroll, my successes or failures, fame or pain, what other people think of me or say about me, my circumstances, or my position. Attitude . . . keeps me going or cripples my progress. It alone fuels my fire or assaults my hope. When my attitudes are right, there's no barrier too high, no valley too deep, no dream too extreme, no challenge too great for me.

The next twelve chapters are devoted to examining the bad attitudes we have. *All eight billion people on this planet have every one of these bad attitudes.* Yes, that includes you and me. It's just a matter of the degree to which we view life these various ways. These bad attitudes are the internal mental obstacles blocking us from having a more meaningful and abundant life. After we explore these bad attitudes, we are going to examine twelve of the best attitudes we can have in life, attitudes that improve our psychological, relational, and spiritual well-being. Working on moving away from our bad attitudes toward the good ones will free us up to fulfill the old Army slogan: "Be all that you can be."

A pat on the back before we go any further. You didn't have to buy this book. That you bought it says there is something in you that wants more in life than the external world of people, places, and things can give you. You have a sense that there is something you can do about your internal world that can make your life better. That, my friend, is a wonderful thing and I am going to do everything I can to help you improve that part of you.

Think About It

1. To what degree have you bought into the pop psychology ideas that attitude is everything, your attitude determines your altitude, and your attitude should be positive?

2. How have the other factors mentioned (nature, nurture, and the nonphysical) impacted your life?

3. Do you accept the idea that even in an experience as horrible as a concentration camp attitude is important for whether or not you survive?

.

The Toxic Twelve

Chapter 2

Wah, Wah, Wah: A Complaining Attitude

This is the true joy in life, the being used for a purpose recognized by yourself as a mighty one; the being thoroughly worn out before you are thrown on the scrap heap; the being a force of nature instead of a feverish, selfish little clod of ailments and grievances complaining that the world will not devote itself to making you happy.

—George Bernard Shaw

I loathe my very life, therefore I will give free rein to my complaint and speak out in the bitterness of my soul.

—Job 10:1

We live in a world that seems to have turned whining, moaning, and complaining into a new art form. At the fitness club where I work out, all some members do is complain ad nauseum about things around the club that aren't to their liking. I must confess that I sometimes join in with them, complaining about the soap dispensers not being refilled fast enough, the hot tub not being hot enough, there being too much trash in the locker room . . . I think you get the point. A lot of us have expectations that are way too high when it comes to the kind of service we think we are entitled to in life.

Look, I'm all for making valid complaints about things that aren't being handled right. If you haven't seen your waiter for fifteen minutes, no one is at the check-out register for you to pay for your groceries, or there is never any soap in the soap dispensers at your fitness club, you need to bring it to the attention of the powers that be. My focus here is on the *whining* we do about the things we have no business whining about.

Some people even complain when they are on vacation. I pulled this off the internet for your reading pleasure: "25 Unbelievably Ridiculous Holiday Complaints People Have Really Made." Let me give you what I thought were the ten choicest complaints:

"The ice in my glass melted too quickly."

"It is your duty as a tour operator to advise us of noisy or unruly guests before we travel."

"Nobody told us the sand would be hot. It was almost impossible to walk on it."

"I only got two toilet paper rolls per day."

"We booked a trip to a water park but nobody told us we had to bring our swimming suits and towels."

"I was bitten by a mosquito. Nobody said they could bite."

"The sand on the beach was whiter than the brochure."

"We had to line up outside to catch our boat and there was no air-conditioning."

"Nobody told us there would be fish in the water. The children were scared."

"The sandy beach was too sandy."

Can you imagine? I'm sure tour guides and hotel and cruise ship operators want to pull their hair out when they hear these kinds of complaints. It probably makes them want to get out of the tourist business altogether. It reminds me of the time I was on a bus tour with my wife, Holly, in England and we were going to see Stonehenge. I tilted my chair back to relax and the two ladies behind me, a mother and daughter combo from the states, immediately complained that I couldn't do that. Holly grabbed my arm and gave me a "stay calm" look before I could enlighten these two women about what I could and couldn't do given that I had paid for the bus tour just like them. Not wanting to ruin the trip, I kept my thoughts to myself and let their complaint slide. I did pray that one of the stones at Stonehenge would fall on both of them when we got there.

A World Full of Complainers

We're all complainers to a certain degree and have a bad case of the "wah-wah-wahs" as we go through life. Our tendency to complain is so bad that we even do it about what are called "first-world problems." I came across this list of "the top 50 first-world problems" on the internet recently. Here are twenty things off the list that people complain about: 1) having a runny nose; 2) a call from an unknown number; 3) being left on hold when calling a company; 4) receiving a "we missed you" card on your door for a failed parcel delivery; 5) having no wi-fi; 6) having a bad phone signal; 7) wanting to log into an account but you can't remember the password; 8) not finding anything you like when clothes shopping; 9) no one replacing the toilet roll; 10) online deliveries arriving late; 11) blisters from new shoes; 12) your neighbor parking in front of your house; 13) a wardrobe full of clothes but nothing to wear; 14) sitting in front of children on a plane; 15) having so much ice in a drink you can't get to the actual drink; 16) online orders taking too long to arrive; 17) experiencing a power loss that keeps you from watching television or cooking; 18) packaging up and returning clothes you bought on line; 19) running out of hot water; and 20) leaving your phone charger at home. Any of this sound familiar?

You know what surprised me, though? Some people even complained about the term "first-world problems," suggesting that it implies we don't have third-world problems in our country (which we do), that third-world countries don't have first-world problems (which they do), or that it isn't okay for people who live in first-world countries to complain about stuff that isn't right or fair. We certainly live in an age of such absurd political correctness that even a term like this one gets complained about.

There are many things wrong with having a complaining attitude. Let me highlight two. First, it puts you in the victim chair. Eckhart Tolle wisely observed, "When you complain you make yourself a victim. Leave the situation, change the situation, or accept it. All else is madness." Second, when you whine, moan, or complain about something, you unconsciously give yourself permission to sit on your rear end and wait for other people to solve your problems for you. Maya Angelou put it this way: "If you don't like something, change it. If you can't change it, change your attitude. Don't complain." Putting yourself in the victim chair and waiting for other people to solve your problems means you're being a whiner.

Again, I admit to complaining too much myself. Most of the complaining I do is internal, but I'm still being a complainer. Just the other day I was internally griping about the fact that it was raining and I couldn't play golf. Can you imagine? I'm complaining about it raining, which is something we actually needed at the time, because it kept me from going out and playing a round of golf! What a whiner! I should have been thankful it rained and simply found something else to do with my precious time. But, nope, I just bellyached the rest of the day that I didn't have another chance to prove how bad of a golfer I am. Not a good use of my time.

Overcoming a Complaining Attitude

I'm not a big fan of "how to" lists because they tend to be fairly superficial and reductionistic. Plus, they assume people want to get their act together and will put sufficient time and energy into the effort, assumptions that, more often than not, aren't true. Many people want to hang on to their problems because it is too painful to face them and too hard to do anything about them. That being said, I want to be superficial, reductionistic, and assume the best about you by offering some "how to" tips in each chapter related to the specific attitude we're exploring.

If you tend to "wah, wah, wah" all the time, here are some tips for how you could break out of being such a whiney person.

Write Down All Your Complaints. People with a complaining attitude usually don't realize just how much complaining they do. Take a few minutes (some of you will need a few hours) to write down all the things you whine about. Heck, just write a list of complaints you had about *today*. Be more aware of how complaint-minded you are. Maybe that will help you stop whining so much.

Look at Whether or Not Your Complaints are Valid. Sometimes, we actually have something to complain about. Sometimes, we don't. If you did the first assignment I asked you to do and wrote down all your complaints, go back through the list and put a "V" by those that are valid and an "I" beside those that are invalid. This could also help you stop complaining so much about how things are going in life.

Use the Rubber Band Technique. Get a thick rubber band and put it around your wrist. Every time you internally or externally complain, whether it is valid or not, pull the rubber band back as far as you can and let her fly. Here, we are going to use the principles of operant conditioning to shape your complaining spirit.

Give Others Three Compliments for Every One Complaint. Complainers usually can give others input on the hundred things they are doing wrong for every positive thing they are doing right. Don't give yourself permission to utter a (valid) complaint until you have paid the person three valid compliments.

When You Complain, Give the Person Specific Actions They Can Take to Make Things Right. Anyone can complain *in general*. It takes a healthy person to be clear about what specifically needs to be done to address their complaint. The other day, I was at a restaurant and ordered a turkey sandwich. When I got my sandwich, there was no turkey in it. All I did was ask them to put turkey in turkey sandwich so that we were clear as to what it would take for me to be a happy, satisfied customer.

There are numerous other ways to overcome a complaining attitude. Try these on for size and see if they help. The more we can break free from a complaining spirit, the better off all of us will be. And, we avoid falling into what George Bernard Shaw warned us about at the top of the chapter, being "a feverish, selfish little clod of ailments and grievances complaining that the world will not devote itself to making you happy."

Some Final Thoughts

In closing, I want to challenge all of us to forbid ourselves from *ever* complaining about *anything* the *rest* of our lives. If something is bugging us, let's ask the people involved to do something about it. Whether it's a first-, second-, or third-world problem, let's stop whining like little babies and maturely request a specific action to be taken that will help go from "problem" to "problem solved."

Regardless of the severity of a given problem, *let's stop complaining about it*! If others won't help us and the problem doesn't go away, at least we handled it with some class and dignity. People hear a request a lot better than they hear a complaint. Let's help them and ourselves out by *putting all our complaints in the form of a request*. I think we'll find that the rest of the world starts listening a lot better and will be willing to more things to help our problems get resolved.

Think About It

1. What kinds of situations do you find yourself whining or complaining about?

2. When you complain about things, do you find yourself waiting on others to solve your problem for you or do you do what you can to resolve the situation?

3. What is currently bugging you in life and what do you need to do about it?

Chapter 3

I'm Better Than You:
A Condescending Attitude

It's very hard not to be condescending when you're explaining something to an idiot.

—Bill Maher

The Pharisee stood by himself and prayed: "God, I thank you that I am not like other people—robbers, evildoers, adulterers—or even like this tax collector."

—Luke 18:11

We live in a world where people can be fairly condescending in how they treat us. People can be condescending if they are smarter than you, more talented than you, more moral than you, wealthier than you, prettier or handsomer than you, or have a greater position of power or prestige than you.

This reminds me of the time I worked as a waiter at a Mexican restaurant. At the time, I had already finished an undergraduate degree and master's degree in psychology and was working on my PhD in counseling psychology at the University of Texas. While the vast majority of the customers I served were respectful and appreciative, there were a few who had the condescending attitude, "You're just a waiter," and treated me like they were doing me a favor allowing me to serve them.

I'll never forget one couple. They spent *three hours* at one of my tables, ran me ragged, barked orders at me, and never once said "thanks" when I brought them anything. On top of that, they left without leaving a tip.

That was the final straw. I did something I had never done before—I followed them out of the restaurant and asked in my best passive-aggressive voice, "Was there something wrong with your service?" The guy grunted back, "No," to which I responded, "Well, I was just wondering because you sat at my table for three hours, ran me like a dog, treated me like dirt, and didn't leave a tip." Upon saying that, I turned around in a huff and stormed back into the restaurant.

The guy, not taking too kindly to my feedback, followed me back into the restaurant and started yelling at my manager about how I had treated him. The manager was a great guy who took good care of his staff, and he proceeded to tell the guy to never come back to the restaurant again. Needless to say, it meant a great deal to me the manager had my back and wasn't going to allow customers to treat his wait staff in a disrespectful and condescending manner. I would have worked for free for him after that. I didn't, but I would have.

All of us can be condescending toward others, especially when we feel the other person is beneath us in some way. Let me share a story about this that made the national news.

The Beautiful Sports Reporter and the Plain Parking Lot Attendant

A story came out a few years ago about a network sports reporter who had a pretty bad reaction to a tow lot attendant. The sports reporter was none too happy that her car had been towed, and she let the parking lot attendant know it.

After retrieving her car, she gave the unsuspecting attendant an earful on her way out. When what happened came to light, this reporter was suspended for a week by her sports network for losing her cool. Among the demeaning insults she hurled at the parking lot attendant were things like "I'm in the news, sweetheart, I will f**king sue this place," "I'm on television and you're in a f**king trailer, honey," "Maybe if I was missing some teeth, they would hire me, huh?" "I wouldn't work at a scumbag place like this," and "Lose some weight, baby girl." The sports reporter was later ashamed of her behavior, saying, "In an intense and stressful moment, I allowed my emotions to get the best of me and said some insulting and regrettable things. I am so sorry for my actions and will learn from this mistake."

My initial reaction to the story was to have a condescending attitude toward this reporter's condescending attitude. I thought to myself, "How arrogant of her as a college educated, talented, highly paid, and attractive person to put this other woman down just because she was none of the above! She ought to be ashamed of herself!" But, after I noodled on it for a while, I started thinking about all the condescending things I have said to people when they weren't treating me the way I wanted to be treated. Unlike the sports reporter, my condescending attitude toward others hasn't ever been caught on video and exposed to the nation. I ended up feeling compassion for this reporter having "been there and done that" in my own condescending mistreatment of my fellow human beings.

Before we move on to the next section, I want to speak to the issue of being condescending *intellectually* toward others. We are in a time in our country where there is more bile and vitriol than ever before when it comes to how differently we see things. When you look at how most people react to those "on the other side of the aisle," you could get the impression that we view others as not having two neurons to rub together when it comes to the opinion they have or view they hold.

Anthony de Mello wisely observed, "Of what use is it to be tolerant of others if you are convinced that you are right and everyone who disagrees with you is wrong? That isn't tolerance but condescension." We seem to be living in a period when disagreeing automatically leads to assuming the other person is wrong and doesn't have anything of insight or intellectual value to offer in shaping the views of others.

This is especially bad when it comes to our political disagreements. There seems to be very little tolerance these days for people to disagree with each other's political views without nine kinds of hell breaking loose. There seems to be very little humility about coming together and reasoning with each other about what the best solution to a given problem might be, one we could all get behind. The intellectual condescension going on in government is tearing our country apart, and we desperately need people on both sides of the aisle to come forward and unite us. There are lots of people on both sides of a disagreement who are smart and have a lot of good ideas—we need to spend more time respecting that fact and listening more deeply to each other.

Overcoming a Condescending Attitude

If you find yourself looking down your nose at others a tad too often, here are some tips I hope you will find helpful for overcoming a condescending attitude.

Always Look for How a Person is Better Than You in Some Way. When we have a condescending attitude, we usually focus on how we are superior to the other person—looks, intelligence, money, personality, character traits, accomplishments, etc. Each time you run into someone, try to size them up for how they might be better than you in some way. I'm going to speak out of the other side of my mouth later on when I challenge you to quit comparing yourself to others, but, for now, let's address our condescending attitude by looking for how others are better than we are in terms of what they bring to the table.

Count Your Many Blessings. If you are better than someone in a particular way, try to be thankful for it being true. Because people are extremely complex and their life experiences are so varied, we have no idea why they might not possess some of the qualities or blessings we do. Thank your lucky stars or God in heaven when you have been blessed with more intelligence, talent, or ability than the average Joe or Jane on the street. After all, your talents and abilities didn't come from you (they came from God), so why would you be arrogant about them?

Have Compassion About People's Situations. The sports reporter who tore into the tow lot attendant didn't seem to have much compassion for what this woman's life was like. Do any of us "have nots" want to be treated in a hateful and condescending way by the "haves" of the world? Wouldn't we like the "haves" of the world to have some compassion and understanding about why we're in the job we're in, why we can't afford to get our teeth fixed, why we don't have a college degree, and the like? Let's try to have compassion (not pity but empathy and sympathy) toward our fellow human beings given the difficult situation some of they are in.

Don't Think Because You're Better Than Someone in a Particular Way You Are Better as a Human Being. Being better at certain things or more successful at a given endeavor doesn't make you better as a human being. Every human being is fearfully and wonderfully made by God. As a result, we all have exactly the same worth and value. Whether you are the CEO of a company or the guy or gal who empties their wastebasket, hold your head up high when you are around others, given that you have worth and value just like they do.

Look for Feelings of Insecurity That Make You Look Down Your Nose at Others. Feelings of superiority are certainly a factor in why we have a condescending attitude toward others, but it is important to realize that sometimes it comes from a deep-seated feeling of inferiority. Why would any of us look down at another person if we truly understand that we have worth and bring certain talents, abilities, and skills to the table each day? Take a few minutes to ask yourself what you feel insecure about that you would falsely prop up your sense of self by looking down on others.

I hope these tips are helpful to you. I know they are easier-said-than-done ways to overcome a condescending attitude, but they are doable and will make your life better.

Some Final Thoughts

I hope all of us will commit to overcoming a condescending attitude toward others about how smart, educated, talented, attractive, famous, admired, powerful, moral, or monied any of us might be. People, in general, already feel bad enough about themselves. No one should be treated in a condescending manner by another human being—it's only pouring salt in an already deep wound. Most of us struggle with strong feelings of worthlessness and inferiority, and we need each other to help us grow out of feeling this way, not make it worse.

May I encourage all of us to look out for ways to affirm others, be thankful for the talents and abilities God gave us, have compassion that the playing field isn't level when it comes to where people sometimes end up in life, remind ourselves that all human beings have worth, and work harder on dealing with the inner insecurities that would lead us to put another human being down. There is no other healthy way to live when dealing with others.

Think About It

1. What are some areas of life where you have a condescending attitude toward others?

2. Is there a specific person in your life you have treated in a condescending manner? In what way have you been condescending toward them?

3. How does it feel when others are condescending toward you?

Chapter 4

I'm the King of the World: A Cocky Attitude

It's hard to be humble when you're as great as I am.

—Muhammad Ali

Those who think they know something
do not yet know as they ought to know.

—1 Corinthians 8:2

I used to love watching the television show *American Idol*. The most cringe-worthy moments for me were when a contestant would come into the room to audition for the judges with an arrogant attitude about their ability to sing, only to fall flat on their face because they couldn't carry a tune in a bucket. It's one thing to come into an audition room confident that you can sing well because you actually have the talent to back it up, and quite another to walk in acting like you're Celine Dion or Luciano Pavarotti when the sound of your voice makes people's ears bleed and dogs bark.

One of the foulest smelling attitudes you can have in life is a cocky one. Being cocky basically means you're *overly* self-confident. A cocky athlete is confident about their athletic ability beyond what they are actually capable of doing. A person who is cocky on an intellectual level thinks they are always right and that their opinion is always better than everyone else's, even when their intellectual abilities don't back it up. A person who is cocky occupationally is overly confident that they bring more talent and ability to a company or organization than they actually do.

In interpersonal relationships, cockiness is a real killer. It's a killer because when you think more highly of yourself than you ought, you feel like you're doing the other person a favor to be in your presence. There is a line in the song, "Hard Habit to Break," by the group, Chicago, that speaks to this: "I was acting as if you were lucky to have me, doing you a favor, I hardly knew you were there."

In political debates, cockiness is what often leads people to not listen to each other. A cocky politician is so sure they are right that they can't entertain the possibility the other side might have something of value to say. A cocky attitude in a political debate shuts your ears off and keeps the discussion from being one where everyone's views are respected.

In sports, a cocky attitude is what often leads to a stunning defeat. A team that steps out on the field of competition *overly* confident they are going to win can sometimes get their hat handed to them. The USA hockey team's upset of the Soviet Union in the 1980 Lake Placid Olympics, the "Miracle on Ice," may be one of the most striking examples. No one expected a young, inexperienced group of college hockey players to beat the great Soviet Union, a team of grizzled veterans who had won one world championship and Olympic gold medal after another. But, win they did and had us all believing in miracles. An overly confident, prideful attitude may have been the main reason for the Soviet Union's great fall.

I want to mention one other kind of cockiness that far too many of us carry around inside—moral cockiness. There are some of us who, however unconsciously, believe we are morally superior to others. This is going to date me, but *Saturday Night Live* used to do a skit where Dana Carvey played "the Church Lady" and acted out this very kind of attitude. During the skit, the Church Lady arrogantly called out the person she interviewed for their sinful and deplorable lifestyle, all while acting like her moral actions were above reproach.

One of the greatest movies of all time, *Star Wars*, had many iconic lines in it. One of my favorites is when Luke Skywalker, after shooting down an enemy plane, proudly proclaims, "Got 'em. I got 'em!," to which Han Solo replies, "Great, kid! Don't get cocky!" When we have success in life, we are more prone to get cocky about our ability, something that can truly lead to our demise. Han Solo was an experienced enough fighter to know that the minute you start getting cocky is the minute you open yourself up to getting blasted. Let me take you into one of the greatest sports examples of how cockiness can cost you, a story that happily seems to be headed in the right direction.

The Cocky Attitude That Went Before Golf's Greatest Fall

He was a golf prodigy, introduced to the game by his father before he turned two. He appeared on *The Mike Douglas Television Show* when he was three to display his golf skills. He broke eighty at the age of eight and seventy at the age of twelve (par is usually seventy-two). He won six Junior World Golf Championships, three US Junior Championships, turned professional at the age of twenty, ascended to number one in the world golf rankings less than a year after turning pro, the top-ranked golfer in the world for 264 consecutive weeks in one stretch and 281 weeks in another, the PGA Player of the Year eleven times, the world's most marketable athlete, and the only athlete other than LeBron James to be named Sportsman of the Year by *Sports Illustrated* twice. Eldrick "Tiger" Woods was truly the king of the golf world from the time he turned pro in 1996 to the time he took a self-imposed hiatus from golf in December of 2009, when it all fell apart.

On Thanksgiving night 2009, Tiger's world came crashing down. His wife at the time, Elin Norgren, discovered that Tiger had been cheating on her. She threw his phone at him, chipped his two front teeth, chased him out of their mansion with one of his golf clubs, followed him in a golf cart to where he had crashed into a fire hydrant in their subdivision, broke out the back window of his car with a golf club, and asked neighbors who had been awakened by all the ruckus to help her out. Tiger, who had taken Vicodin and Ambien to help him sleep, lay on the ground slipping in and out of consciousness until EMS and the police arrived. Tiger later confessed to having cheated on his wife with a slew of pornstars, strippers, and call girls. Tiger checked into rehab to be treated for sex addiction, was dropped by many of his sponsors, and unceremoniously fell from grace in the golf world. Tiger and Elin tried to save their marriage but ended up divorcing in 2010. Years of psychological, moral, and physical rehab followed as Tiger tried to put his life back together.

I don't say all this to rub Tiger's past in his face but only to make a point that is true about *all of us*: No matter what level of success or notoriety we achieve, we can become cocky and arrogant about it and bring everything crashing down around us. Tiger Woods got too full of himself given all of his amazing accomplishments and ended up feeling entitled to all the perks that worldwide fame and success offered. He damaged his marriage, his family, his reputation, the game of golf, his sponsors, and his status in the world of golf, all because his cockiness overtook him and led him down the path to personal ruin.

Tiger's story appears to be headed toward a happy ending. Because of the public humiliation from his affairs coming to light and a series of significant back and knee injuries, Tiger experienced a great deal of failure and setback. He got a huge piece of humble pie served to him by his bad decisions but has responded well to it. Years of struggle and pain seems to have taken the cockiness out of Tiger and that has been replaced with humility, a *healthy* sense of confidence, being more engaged with others, and dropping his sense of entitlement. Tiger is more engaged with his children, works collaboratively with his ex-wife to raise them properly, gets along better with his fellow professional golfers, treats the fans better, and isn't near as dismissive as he used to be in interviews.

The Tiger Woods saga recently reached a very positive crescendo when he won the 2019 Masters in dramatic fashion, putting a nice finishing touch to his comeback from moral, psychological, and physical setbacks. Given that I'm a huge Tiger fan, I couldn't be happier for him. I only hope he will stay humble and not fall back into feeling entitled to all the worldly perks that go with great success. People are already lavishing praise on Tiger as if he is God's gift to the planet, and I hope he will take all that with a huge grain of salt. If I were Tiger's psychologist, I would say to him what Han Solo said to Luke Skywalker, "Great, kid! Don't get cocky!"

We're no different than Tiger Woods deep down in our fallen heart of hearts. We all have a cocky, arrogant, full-of-ourselves person inside that thinks he or she is better than everyone else walking the planet. Don't get defensive about that or act like it's not true. We all do our own version of being the narcissistic jerk who is grandiose about our own awesomeness while acting like others are peons. Tiger fell into that, and we fall into it as well. Hopefully, like Tiger, we can mature and come out of it.

Overcoming a Cocky Attitude

If you want to overcome a cocky attitude, here are some tips for how you might want to go about doing something about it.

28

Admit Your Mistakes. Cocky people have a hard time admitting they are human. Sometimes, you can't pry an apology out of their mouth with a crowbar. When you screw up, just admit it. Otherwise, you're feeding your cockiness rather than fighting it.

Gladly Give Credit Where Credit is Due. Cocky people tend to take full credit for their accomplishments. When you achieve something great or almost-great, make sure you acknowledge all the people who contributed to your accomplishment and the God of the universe for giving you talent and ability to do it.

Remember Your Limitations. Cocky people tend to think they either don't have any flaws or that their flaws are minor. We are all finite, fallen humans beings who mess things up all the time because, unlike God, we aren't all-knowing, all-powerful, and everywhere at once. Don't dwell on your limitations, just don't forget you have them.

Compliment Others and Genuinely Mean It. Cocky people are usually looking for a compliment from others but are pretty stingy about giving them. Be on the lookout for how to compliment other people regarding the talents, strengths, and abilities they have rather than looking for them to compliment you about yours. Go through each day looking to pass out as many genuine compliments as you can so that you help others feel better about themselves.

Remember People's Names and Show Interest in Their Lives. I have a pretty bad memory for names, especially if I don't see someone on a regular basis. Nevertheless, we need to remember people's names, call them by their name, and spend time, even if it just a few minutes, learning more about them and their life. Cocky people tend to want you to remember their name and show an interest in their life but often don't return the favor.

There are a million more tips I could give you for how to overcome a cocky attitude. These five are worth your consideration and will help you become a healthier person if you implement them. As I said earlier, we all have a tendency to be cocky in life, thinking more highly of ourselves than we should. Don't let yourself do that; you'll only bring about your own downfall.

Some Final Thoughts

There is a popular expression these days, "Don't get over your skis." What this means to me is that we are not to be *overly* confident about what we can accomplish in light of what our talents, abilities, training, experience, and efforts will actually allow.

The first time I went skiing, I spent the morning in ski school. It would have been cocky of me to head from beginner's ski school to the black diamond slopes (the most difficult slopes of all) after spending only a couple of hours being shown how to stay upright and not impale myself or others with a ski pole. Had I been cocky enough to try the black diamond slopes after my introductory lesson, I most certainly would have had a painful encounter with the ground, other skiers, and the trees lining the ski run.

A cocky attitude damages your relationships with others, how well you perform, and makes you insufferable to be around. Cockiness might draw people to you in the beginning, but it is going to cost you in the long run. Life will certainly give you trophies along the way, but it will just as gladly take them back if you fall into being cocky.

Please, drop the cocky attitude. Humble yourself by remembering that the talents and abilities you have didn't come from you, they came from God. Humble yourself by admitting your mistakes when you make them. Humble yourself by giving credit to others for the helpful role they played in your success. Humble yourself by complimenting other people for how good they are at things. Humble yourself by remember people's names and showing an interest in their lives. And, humble yourself by never losing sight of your limitations as a human being who can't go from beginner lessons to black diamond slopes the same day.

It's okay to be confident about the talents and abilities you have. Just make sure you stay humble about them being on loan from God and to be used for other people's enjoyment and betterment.

Think About It

1. What areas of your life have you had a cocky attitude about (where you thought more highly of yourself than was warranted)?

2. Who in your life would you say has the cockiest attitude, what area of life are they cocky about (again, think more highly of themselves than they should), and how has that impacted your relationship with them?

3. Have you noticed people in your life reacting to your cockiness, and, if so, what was their reaction like?

Chapter 5

No One Ever Does Anything Right:
A Critical Attitude

> It is not the critic who counts, nor the man who points out how the strong man stumbled or where the doer of deeds could have done them better. The credit belongs to the man who is actually in the arena; whose face is marred by dust and sweat and blood; who strives valiantly . . . who knows the great enthusiasms, the great devotions, and spends himself in a worthy cause; who, at best, knows the triumph of high achievement and who, at the worst, if he fails, at least fails while daring greatly, so that his place shall never be with those cold and timid souls who know neither victory or defeat.
>
> —Theodore Roosevelt

> Do not judge, or you too will be judged. For in the same way you judge others, you will be judged, and with the measure you use, it will be measured to you.
>
> —Matthew 7:1–2

Comedian Jeff Foxworthy is famous for his "You might be a redneck if . . ." jokes. Some of my favorites are "If you've ever made change in the offering plate, you might be a redneck," "You might be a redneck if the blue book value of your truck goes up and down depending on how much gas it has in it," "If your dad walks you to school because you're in the same grade, you might be a redneck," "You may be a redneck if you think you are an entrepreneur because of the 'Dirt for Sale' sign in the front yard," and "If you think that Dom Perignon is a mafia leader, you might be a redneck."

Let me suggest that "You might be a critical person if . . .":

- you constantly pick yourself and others apart
- you can't take a compliment or give one
- you frequently make moral evaluations of others
- you can't tolerate other people being different from you
- people are afraid to share things with you
- you allow very little room for human imperfection
- you negatively judge others in an effort to elevate yourself
- very few, if any, things in life are enjoyable
- you're losing friends
- you focus on the negative traits of others rather than their positive ones
- nothing is ever good enough
- you're black and white, all or nothing in how you think
- you jump to conclusions before you have all the facts
- you justify criticism as "keeping it real" and "being a straight shooter"

Not a fun list to go through, is it? It's painful, but I identify with way too many of these aspects of having a critical attitude. Let me give you an example.

The way people drive makes me want to pull my hair out. I say this acknowledging that four things from the above list come into play for me about people's driving—I focus on the negative driving habits of others, allow no room for human imperfection, am black and white in my evaluations, and the way they drive is never good enough. From my hyper-critical perspective, people rarely use their turn indicator, drive the speed limit (they go either too fast or too slow), pay enough attention (because they are usually on their cell phones), back far enough off your bumper, or come to a complete stop at stop signs (my three adult children are fond of saying, "Dad, no cop, no stop"). You don't have to be a psychologist to see why this particular mental health professional is a nut case when driving on the highway.

Let me take you into my counseling office and talk about a couple I worked with, one of whom criticized her way out of a marriage that was actually a reasonably good one and could have not only lasted but flourished.

The Wife That Wouldn't Stop Criticizing Her Husband

Before you get upset, I want you to know that I am not suggesting it is always the wife who is critical of her husband. I have counseled hundreds of couples over the years and have found men and women, in general, to be equally prone to criticizing each other in marriage. That being said, I want to take you into my office about a particular couple I counseled to drive home the point that a critical attitude is going to cost you a relationship regardless of your gender. Names and identifying characteristics have been changed to protect the guilty.

Helen had been married to her husband, Neil, for seventeen years. They had three children, all girls, whom they dearly loved. Helen and Neal met in college, fell in love, and got married after six months of dating. To hear them tell it, there were no major red flags during brief the time they dated, nothing that suggested they were with the wrong person or that they shouldn't get married.

To hear Neil tell it, it wasn't long after they married that Helen started in on him, frequently criticizing pretty much everything about him. Helen was an unending source of negative input for Neil and never seemed to have a kind word to say about him. From her perspective, Neil didn't give her enough attention or affection ("The only reason he ever hugs me is because he wants to have sex"), wasn't helpful around the house ("He never lifts a finger to help"), didn't interact with their children enough ("I'm basically doing all the parenting"), wasn't outgoing in social situations ("He's way too quiet and introspective"), didn't make enough money ("We're never going to live in a nice place"), wasn't a good lover ("He doesn't light my fire in the bedroom"), and didn't like the friends he hung around with ("They're all a bunch of losers"). In Helen's eyes, Neil had few, if any, redeeming qualities. To deal with her unhappiness, Helen demanded she and Neal go to counseling as a last-ditch effort to save their marriage.

I've been in this kind of counseling situation quite often during my years as a psychologist, where one person is super-critical of the other, doesn't see anything about the other that they like or admire, and pours on the criticism day after day. Helen wasn't about to let me give her any feedback on her flaws and defects because she didn't think she had any. She wanted me to fix her husband.

I've got to hand it to Neil. He took all of Helen's feedback to heart, changed many of the things she wanted him to change, and spent the six months doing nothing but maritally delivering the goods. He did a masterful job of taking away Helen's criticisms by not giving her much, if anything, to criticize.

Nevertheless, and much to his dismay, the criticisms kept coming. No matter how much Neil stepped up to the plate and became the man Helen wanted him to be, she was never happy. Nothing he did was ever enough.

During the last session we had together, Neil came in, stopped Helen from dominating the session, and let her know that he had filed for divorce and that she was going to be served with divorce papers later that day. He had used the previous six months to call her bluff by making all the changes she asked him to make and decided he was not going to spend the rest of his life letting her criticize him while running from her own defects. Neil followed through on his decision to end the marriage, and they are no longer husband and wife.

I tell you this story because I have personally witnessed hundreds of times just how deadly and destructive a critical spirit is in relationships. If you don't take the plank out of our own eye in dealing with others because you are too busy criticizing the speck in theirs, you are going to be the primary reason things don't work out and may very well spend the rest of your life alone. A critical spirit in life is a killer—it kills the spirit of those around you and it atrophies your own spirit in the process.

Overcoming a Critical Attitude

Here are some tips I hope you will find useful in overcoming a critical attitude. Give them a try in learning how to back off criticizing yourself and others.

Adjust Your Expectations. An overly critical person typically has expectations of themselves and others that are *way too high*! For some overly critical people, the standard is perfection. When that's the case, it's no wonder that they are constantly criticizing everything and everyone. Adjust your standards to a level appropriate for *human beings*, all of whom go through life noticeably mistake-prone and as a constant "work in progress."

Keep your Eyes on the Positive. Whether it is toward yourself or others, try to pay more attention to what you and others do right, not what they do wrong. Purposely be on the lookout for how people act in a "close enough for horseshoes" manner in doing things well. Affirm others when they do a good job, and try to tap the brakes on giving them negative feedback.

Ask Yourself Whether You Need to Say Anything at All. Just because you noticed a mistake or flaw doesn't automatically mean you're supposed to comment on it. If your motives are bad (you just want to shame or embarrass someone), you most definitely aren't the one who is supposed to say anything. Be careful to never presume to be judge, jury, and executioner toward those who make mistakes.

Work Hard to Not Take People's Mistakes Personally. Sometimes the reason we criticize others is that they did something we found hurtful. When that happens, we have a tendency to "personalize" their actions as if they are about us somehow. People's mistakes are about them, not about us. Try not to take people's miscues that are hurtful to you personally.

Don't Criticize, Ask for Change in Behavior. You never need to criticize another person's behavior. All you need to do is ask them to improve it. Push yourself to take a critical thought your having about someone and put it in the form of a request for how they can change what they are doing.

Some Final Thoughts

A critical attitude, whether it is aimed at yourself or others, destroys everyone in its path. If nothing you or others do is ever good enough or right, you're pretty much going to be a miserable human being and make others miserable along the way. That's why I opened the chapter with the quote from Theodore Roosevelt. He's right to say that it isn't the critic who counts but the person out on the battlefield who strives valiantly in the name of giving themselves to a worthy cause. Ah, if I could take that attitude out on a golf course, I could be playing on the Senior's Tour (not really, that's a cocky attitude).

I want to challenge all of us to stop being critical of ourselves and others. If we are going to put ourselves or others "under the microscope," let's do it solely for the purpose of evaluating what we can improve, not to put anyone down or make them feel small. Given that many of us feel small enough already, we certainly don't need to criticize ourselves or anyone else as we go through life. Let's get off our own backs and the backs of others by refusing to criticize anymore. Let's only say something when it will leave us or them better off.

Think About It

1. In what ways are you critical of yourself?

2. In what ways are you critical of others?

3. How could you give yourself or others constructive feedback that leads to improvement rather than scathing criticisms that lead to hurt?

Chapter 6

You Disgust Me: A Contemptuous Attitude

Contempt is the weapon of the weak and a defense
against one's own despised and unwanted feelings.

—Alice Miller

Whoever shows contempt for his neighbor lacks sense,
but a man with understanding keeps silent.

—Proverbs 11:2

Dr. John Gottman is one of the world's foremost marriage researchers. His book *The Seven Principles for Making Marriage Work* has sold zillions of copies, more than all of mine combined (something I have great bitterness and resentment about), and helped couples around the world improve their relationships. Dr. Gottman came up with many important findings in his research on relationships, one of the most well-known being what he calls "the Four Horsemen of the Apocalypse."

The Four Horsemen of the Apocalypse are the four most damaging communication styles a couple can engage in, styles of interacting that dramatically increase the chances a relationship won't last. The Four Horsemen of the Apocalypse are: criticism, contempt, defensiveness, and stonewalling. Guess which of the four is the single greatest predictor of divorce (if you get this wrong in light of the focus of this chapter, you must not be paying enough attention). Yes, that's right, contempt. Contempt is the worst of the four horsemen and the strongest predictor that a couple is headed for divorce.

I think contempt is more than just a communication style. I think it is a heart attitude some people have where they actually feel disgusted by the flaws and defects in other people. Some people have a contemptuous attitude as they go through life, one that expresses itself in name calling, cutting humor, sarcasm, eye-rolling, giving others the cold shoulder, and being harsh and attacking. Contempt toward a person reflects negative sentiments that have been "cooking" for a long time and often leads to verbally attacking the person's sense of self.

Aesop's aphorism "Familiarity breeds contempt" certainly comes into play in a lot of relationships. The idea here is that the more you get to know someone, the more you focus on what is wrong with them. The more you see what is wrong with them, the more likely you are to experience contempt for the person, especially if their defects have been hurtful to you. Even though it is a fictional account of a marriage, let me take you into a marriage that became, at its core, a marriage of contempt.

The Roses

One of the more well-known black comedies about the catastrophic effect of contempt in marriage is *The War of the Roses*. Oliver and Barbara meet at an antique auction when they are college students, fall head-over-heels in love, get married, and set up life in Washington, D.C., he as a lawyer and she as a homemaker and, later on, fine dining expert. As they come to know each other (familiarity), they grow in their hostile and negative feelings (contempt).

Oliver can't stand Barbara's middle-class background, cat, spending habits, obsession with remodeling their home, and how she spoils their children by giving them treats that lead to both of them being overweight. Barbara can't stand Oliver's laugh, dog, obsession with his sports car, and that he is a controlling, self-centered, and dismissive workaholic.

Over the course of the movie, Oliver humiliates Barbara at a dinner party she is hosting (out of decorum, I won't tell you how, but it's gross), runs over her cat (accidentally), and breaks her expensive dishware and figurines (on purpose). Barbara returns the favor by locking Oliver in their sauna where he nearly dies from heatstroke, running over his sports car with her truck, and serving him paté that she implies was made from his dog who had gone missing, and not coming to the hospital when he has what he thinks is a heart attack but turns out to be a bad case of indigestion.

A bitter divorce ensues. Neither will compromise on what to do with their home and all its belongings, and (spoiler alert) they end up causing each other's death. I told you it was a black comedy, didn't I? If you are the least bit concerned that you may have a contemptuous attitude toward your partner, a close friend, your boss, or a work associate, watch *The War of the Roses*. English write Samuel Johnson once said, "Contempt is a kind of gangrene which, if it seizes one part of a character, corrupts all the rest by degrees." *The War of the Roses* proves him to be right in a way that will make you both laugh and cry.

Alice Miller is correct to say, "Contempt is the weapon of the weak and a defense against one's own despised and unwanted feelings." I would just expand her statement to say that we not only feel contempt toward our own "despised and unwanted feelings" but our despised and unwanted thoughts and actions.

We all have some degree of inner contempt toward ourselves, ways we are disgusted not only by the feelings we have but by the thoughts and behaviors we experience. Because we need to take a psychological break from the contempt we feel toward ourselves, we often redirect our contempt in the direction of others and find their feelings, attitudes, and actions contemptible. When we feel contempt toward them, we end up treating them the way Oliver and Barbara treated each other—cruelly and sadistically.

One of the saddest parts of *The War of the Roses* to me was that Oliver didn't seem to have a clue he had contempt toward Barbara and had been treating her so dismissively. When Barbara tells Oliver she wants a divorce, he is dumbfounded given how hard he has worked as a high-powered lawyer to provide a lavish lifestyle for her and their children. Oliver had no clue that his unconscious contempt for his wife had been wounding to her, nor could he understand why she was so filled with contempt in fighting back on how they were going to divide their estate. Contempt has a way of putting blinders on just how badly you can treat the people you love the most.

Sadly, to a certain degree, the Roses are you and me. We all have a person or group of people we feel contempt toward. We all have feelings of disgust toward others that we are largely unaware of that come flooding out of us when they do something we find offensive or immoral. Far too often, we feel contempt toward the sin *and* the sinner. Don't fool yourself, you have contempt in your heart toward someone or something.

Overcoming a Contemptuous Attitude

Feeling contempt toward other human beings is a horrible place to end up, even if it is just toward one person. Here are some tips for how to overcome a contemptuous attitude.

Get the Plank Out of Your Own Eye. Take your focus off the person you have contempt for and spend some time being honest about your own defects. Every single one of us have things about us that are truly bad, darker than we could have ever imagined. We are all in denial about just how big of a mess we are. To switch metaphors, stay in your own backyard—there are some really big weeds there and you have no business looking into other people's backyards until you deal with your own.

Consider the Possibility That What You Feel Contempt Toward Others About Is True About You. We all project our defects and flaws onto others. It just may be the case that what you find so detestable in others is something true about you. Even if the other person has the same bad qualities you do, try to stop projecting your bad qualities onto them and own your less-than-wonderful flaws.

Apologize to the People You Have Contempt Toward and Ask Them to Forgive You. If you want to overcome a contemptuous attitude, you need to own it in front of the person you feel that way toward. You need to look them in the eye and say, "I am embarrassed to admit this, but I feel contempt toward you. I want to own that feeling this way is about me and not you. It is wrong to feel this way toward you. Will you please forgive me for treating you badly? Specifically, will you forgive me for being dismissive in my interactions with you, putting your thoughts and feelings down, and treating you as if you have no redeeming qualities. I am truly sorry that I would have treated you this way and want to repair the damage I have caused."

Ask the Other Person to Tell You What They Don't Like About You. Another way to overcome feelings of contempt toward someone is to get them to say what they don't like about you. You have spent too much time focusing on what you don't like about them, so give them time to non-abusively return the favor. All of us have some unlikeable qualities. If you want to overcome an attitude of contempt, let someone speak truthfully to what your unlikeable qualities are and take their feedback to heart.

Stop Having Contempt for Yourself. The contempt we have toward others is often masking the contempt we feel toward ourselves. Take some time to process the contempt you may feel toward yourself and see if you can start making a distinction between having contempt toward yourself and having contempt for your flaws and defects. Distinguish between you and your behavior. Hate the sin and not the sinner. If you can do that for yourself, you might find it easier to do toward others so that you can hate (strong word) their defects but not hate them as a human being.

I hope these tips are helpful to you in overcoming contempt toward others and yourself. Remember what I told you in chapter 1. You need to *accept* (not like) that you have these bad attitudes, have *compassion* that you think this way given that it is making your life (and other people's lives) harder, remind yourself that you value having the right attitude in life, and stay the course in moving away from bad attitudes like contempt toward good attitudes like compassion and caring.

Some Final Thoughts

John Gottman's work on what makes or breaks intimate relationships has helped millions of people. The fact that he identified contempt as the deadliest killer of relationships should come as no surprise. When a couple comes into my office and either one of them has contempt for the other, I know I have my work cut out for me and that unless he or she moves in the direction of compassion, humility, and forgiveness their relationship is dead in the water.

It's more than heartbreaking when people in a relationship choose the path of contempt rather than the path of compassion and reconciliation. And, this is not just a marriage thing. I have seen sons and daughters hold on to contempt toward parents, siblings hold on to contempt toward each other, former best friends hold on to contempt toward each other, married folks hold on to contempt toward in-laws, and groups of people hold on to contempt for other groups of people. All it ever accomplishes is the destruction of relationships, not an accomplishment to be proud of.

The ultimate problem with contempt is that it will keep you from forgiving others. There is no way you are going to forgive a person you feel contempt toward. A contemptuous heart always gets in the way of being able to forgive others, reconcile with them, and be at peace with them. There's a well-known quote that a few hundred people seem to have taken credit for: "Unforgiveness is like taking poison and hoping the other person dies." You're not only killing the relationship when your contempt toward someone gets in the way of forgiving them, you're killing yourself. Lewis Smedes is right to observe, "To forgive is to set a prisoner free and discover that the prisoner was you."

I leave you with a final quote on forgiveness. Thomas Fuller said, "He that cannot forgive others breaks the bridge over which he must pass himself; for every man has need to be forgiven." Don't forget—because of the selfish things we do, we need forgiveness from others as well. Let's all drop our attitude of contempt so we can forgive and reconcile with each other. We have everything to gain and nothing to lose—except our pride.

Think About It

1. Which person do you feel the most contempt toward and what do you find so displeasing about him or her?

2. How have you, through your actions, expressed contempt toward them?

3. Are you willing to apologize to this person and move in the direction of forgiveness and reconciliation?

Chapter 7

The Sky is Falling: A Catastrophizing Attitude

I've been through some terrible things in my life,
some of which actually happened.

— Mark Twain

Elijah was afraid and ran for his life . . . He came to a broom bush,
sat down under it and prayed that he might die.

— 1 Kings 19:3–4

I don't know if this folk tale is told to children anymore, but I fondly remember from my childhood the story of Chicken Little. I'll play psychologist on myself here for a minute and suggest that I liked the story as a kid
because I strongly identified with the lead character. Let me explain.

Chicken Little is out on a walk one day when an acorn falls from the
sky and bonks her on the head. She immediately assumes the sky is falling
and anxiously goes off to tell the king about what happened. On her way,
she runs into Henny Penny and gets him all stirred up about it. They join
forces in an effort to tell everyone else about the doom that awaits them
and run into Lucky Ducky. They get Lucky Ducky all stirred up about the
fact that the sky is falling and run farther down the road, only to encounter
Foxy Loxy and tell him about the bad news.

There are numerous versions of Chicken Little. One ends tragically
with Foxy Loxy luring Chicken Little, Henny Penny, and Lucky Ducky into

his cave and the three of them never coming out alive. I can't remember if that was the one I read as a child. I hope not.

The happier version of Chicken Little involves them making their way to the king, him taking Chicken Little back to the scene of the crime, a squirrel coming out to ask if anyone had seen the acorn she dropped earlier in the day, and Chicken Little being helped to see that not everything in life is quite the tragedy it might appear to be.

In counseling circles, we talk about a "sky-is-falling" attitude as the tendency to catastrophize, to make things a lot bigger and more threatening than they really are. Let me take you into a more recent children's story to drive this home, one that is quite popular among kiddos these days.

It may go without saying, but I identify with this character as well, having spent most of my life catastrophizing painful or negative events that happen and reacting in an overly anxious and upset way.

Before I go into this story, I want to make sure that you understand what I'm *not* saying in this chapter. I'm not saying that painful things don't happen to us, nor am I saying that some of them are not big. If you have ever lost a loved one, had a painful relationship break-up, a health scare, or major career setback, you know that some events are not only upsetting but rather significant. What I'm saying here is that the tendency to make them even bigger than they are is what can spell our doom in life.

A Really, Really, Really Bad Day

One of my best friends on the planet, someone who knows me well enough to know how much of a "sky is falling" kind of guy I can be, bought me a children's book once. I felt a little bit patronized that he got me a *children's* book, but he truly cares about me and I knew that he was looking out for me in what he did. The name of the book was, *Alexander and the Terrible, Horrible, No Good, Very Bad Day*. If a book was ever written about me, it's this one.

The book is about an especially bad day a young boy named Alexander experiences. From the second Alexander wakes up, he can tell it is going to be a terrible, horrible, no good, very bad day. The chewing gum that was in his mouth when he went to bed is in his hair when he wakes up, he trips on a skateboard and drops his sweater in the sink while the water is running, his brothers find a prize in the breakfast cereal box and he finds nothing but cereal, and he doesn't get a window seat on the way to school and tells everyone he is going to throw up if that happens again.

Not bad enough? Alexander's teacher likes another student's picture of a sailboat better than Alexander's picture of an invisible castle (meaning a picture of nothing), she tells Alexander at singing time that he sings too loud, and she tells him at counting time that he skipped the number sixteen (to which he responds, "Who needs sixteen?"). Alexander's best friend demotes him to being his third best friend, his mother forgets to put a dessert in his lunch bag, he is the only one of his brothers who has a cavity when they go to see their dentist, an elevator door closes on his foot, one of his brothers pushes him into a mud puddle and calls him a crybaby for whining about it, his mother scolds him for being muddy and punching his brother for calling him a crybaby, and he is forced to buy plain white shoes at the shoe store rather than the blues ones with a red stripe that he really wanted.

Still not bad enough? Alexander makes a mess of everything he touches at his father's office, he's served lima beans for dinner even though he hates lima beans, he sees people kissing on television even though he hates people kissing, his bathwater is too hot and he gets soap in his eyes, his marble ends up going down the drain, he is forced to wear the railroad train pajamas he hates, his Mickey Mouse nightlight burns out, he bites his tongue, his brother takes a bed pillow he said Alexander could keep, and the cat wants to sleep with his brother and not him. Clearly, Alexander had a terrible, horrible, no good, very bad day.

Ever feel like that? Ever feel that a day turned out to be a terrible, horrible, no good, very bad thing? Ever feel that way about your life as a whole? If you have, you are falling into what we counselor types call catastrophizing. All of us catastrophize on occasion, but some of us have a catastrophizing attitude. All of this, of course, goes hand in hand with having a complaining attitude. Not only did Alexander catastrophize all the things that happened to him that particular day, but he seemed to do very little else than whine, moan, and complain about his terrible, horrible, no good, very bad day.

Overcoming a Catastrophizing Attitude

We all have a tendency to make things bigger than they really are. Here are some tips for how to overcome the tendency to catastrophize I hope you will find helpful in your efforts to handle things better in life.

Acknowledge There are Difficult Things in Life and That It's Not Wrong to See It That Way. Life is full of difficult and challenging problems, and we don't want to deny that. It's not any better to *minimize* the things that happen to you than it is to *maximize* them. We all need to accept that in this world we will have big, painful things come our way.

Figure Out the "Size" of the Event. If you are going to overcome your tendency to catastrophize, you need to spend more time accurately assessing the true *size* of the event that happened. I give my clients a scale from 5-cent events (the truly small stuff) to $500 events (the major life events like death of a loved one, a serious illness, losing a job, my Longhorns losing to the Sooners). When you find yourself making a mountain out of a molehill, stop and ask yourself where the event objectively falls on this scale.

Avoid Other Catastrophizers. Birds of a feather flock together, and misery loves company. If you have a tendency to catastrophize things, make sure you don't spend too much time around other catastrophizers. Otherwise, you'll come together, stir each other up into a frenzy, and jump off the ledge together. If you want to overcome this particular mindset, you have to steer clear of those who would only fan the flames of your tendency to catastrophize.

Take a Deep Breath and Relax. The tendency to catastrophize stirs up your "fight or flight" physiology, sometimes to the panic level. When you are making things bigger than they actually are, take a deep breath and get your breathing regulated.

Ask Others for Input on How Big a Deal They Think Your Situation Is. Ask some of your closest friends to weigh in on what "size" they think the event is that you are dealing with (using the 5-cent to $500 scale). Average all their responses, and you'll come up with a better sense of where in the grand scheme of things the event falls.

Some Final Thoughts

If you're like me, you find yourself making things much bigger than they really are—a slight from a friend, someone cutting you off in traffic, people showing up late for an appointment, a spouse not following through on something, and the like. It's on us to see the event in its proper size and to talk ourselves down from the edge of the cliff.

Whatever else mental health is all about, it has a lot to do with seeing external events in their proper size. Those of us who catastrophize are going to overreact to the things that happen, be much harder to deal with, and a lot harder to be close to. The next time a 5-cent event happens to you, do yourself a favor: try to have 5 cents worth of emotion. The next time a $500 event happens to you, do yourself a favor and try to have $500 worth of emotion. Remember, objectivity and proportionality.

Think About It

1. What things in your past did you make a bigger deal than they actually were?

2. What things in your present life do you find yourself catastrophizing?

3. When you catastrophize things, how do you react to them?

Chapter 8

I've Got to Have What You Have:
A Covetous Attitude

Covetousness is the greatest of monsters, as well as the root of all evil.

—William Penn

You shall not covet . . .

—Exodus 20:17

C ovet: to desire inordinately (Merriam-Webster). Not a pleasant word, is it? When I think back through my life, I can see a number of things I have coveted. Let me share one from my childhood.

When we were stationed at March Air Force base in California in the early 1960s, there was a kid on base who had a bicycle I wanted so badly I could taste it. It was a Schwinn Stingray. I can't begin to tell you how much I wanted that bike. It was the coolest bike on the planet—white "banana" seat, "butterfly" handlebars, a short frame that looked like the bicycle version of a hot sports car, and a slick back tire. My friend had a candied apple red version. I don't know that I have ever lusted after something like that bicycle my whole life.

One Christmas, my parents asked my brothers and me to give them a list of all the things we wanted. I, of course, only wanted one thing—a Stingray bike. Unbeknownst to me, they were expensive. One ad for the bike during that time period priced them at $49.95. That would be $413.21 adjusted for inflation today. My dad was a captain in the Air Force at the time, and he was struggling to rub two dimes together to take care of our family. There was no way he could spend that much on a Christmas present for one of his sons. Heck, he couldn't afford to spend that much on the entire family.

The big day came and went, and there was no Stingray bike next to the tree. I remember walking outside to collect myself after all the presents had been opened. My dad came out, put his arm around me, and apologized he couldn't get me the bike. I'll never forget him doing that. It meant a lot to me that my dad wanted that bike for me as much as I did.

Now that I'm an adult, I find myself coveting a Corvette Stingray. I guess I have this thing about Stingrays. I tell my family and friends that if they ever win the lottery or become rich and famous, I want them to promise me that the first purchase they make will be a Corvette Stingray for me—candied apple red, please. I want a Corvette Stingray so bad I can taste it. I even thought about renting one for a day, just so I can feel what it is like to drive a car with that much horsepower (my car has two squirrel cages generating squirrelpower that barely allows me to go faster than sixty miles per hour). Yeah, if I could just have a Corvette Stingray, all would be well with my soul and God could take me home.

I bring all this up to talk about a covetous attitude, the attitude we have when we find ourselves wanting something or someone so bad that we feel like we are going to die if we don't have it. We all fall into coveting things in life, every single one of us. And, like I did as a child and now as an adult, we all need to step outside in the fresh air and collect ourselves when what we covet doesn't come our way.

I want you to move away for a moment from whether or not you believe God exists or think the Bible is an accurate record of historical events. Play along with me here as I take you into one of the most iconic stories in the Bible about coveting, an incident in one man's life that changed his circumstances forever.

Coveting Another Man's Wife

King David is one of the most important figures in the Bible. We are first introduced to him when he is young shepherd boy tending his father's flocks. David is said to have killed a lion with his bare hands and chopped down a nine-foot-tall giant with a stone. The Bible also says he was a world-class musician and poet, a highly skilled military leader and warrior, and chosen from among his older brothers to be the future king of Israel when he wasn't old enough to shave. David was the king of the hill, the top of the heap, and the cat's meow of his generation.

Apparently, all that wasn't enough for David. He seemed to have an eye for beautiful women. When he was the king of Israel, David had numerous wives, more than the seven mentioned by name. As if that weren't enough, David had numerous concubines, more than the ten mentioned in the Bible. To say that David had a coveting eye for attractive women would be an understatement.

One evening, when he was supposed to be out on the battlefield fighting bad guys alongside his men, David was walking on the palace roof. He spotted this drop-dead gorgeous woman taking a bath and sent one of his servants to find out her name. David is informed that her name is Bathsheba and that she is married to one of *his* fiercest warriors, Uriah the Hittite. David is supposed to be out on the battled field with Uriah fighting the enemy, and, instead, he is eyeballing his wife.

Things go from bad to worse at this point in the story. Undeterred that she is married to one of his warriors, David has Bathsheba brought to the palace, sleeps with her, and sends her away. Later on, Bathsheba lets David know she is pregnant with his child. To cover his sin, David further compounds the problem by arranging to have Uriah the Hittite killed in battle, ordering that he be put up on the front lines where the fighting is the fiercest. As planned, Uriah is killed in battle and David has Bathsheba brought to the palace to be his wife.

Let's step back from all this for a moment. David is this uber-talented, handsome, successful guy who is the King of Israel. He already has numerous wives and concubines, something God told him not to do. He spots a beautiful woman on a nearby roof taking a bath, finds out who she is, discovers she is married to one of his best soldiers, has her brought over to the palace, has sex with her, is told she is carrying his child, has her husband killed to cover things up, and takes her into his palace as one of his wives. What in the name of all things decent is going on here?

May I suggest that David had a problem that *all of us have—covetousness*. In David's case, he coveted beautiful women. I've spent my life coveting Stingray bikes and cars, whereas David spent his life coveting gorgeous women. You may think I am being too rough on David here. I'm not. Deep in the heart of every man and woman is a covetous monster, and, if we give in to that monster, we are headed for a fall.

It is important to note that coveting has nothing to do with your circumstances. As Charles Ryrie insightfully observed, "One can be covetous when he has little, much or anything between, for covetousness comes from the heart, not from the circumstances of life." And, it is important to note that all coveting is a spiritual phenomenon, not only a secular one. Mark Twain observed, "There is no such thing as material covetousness. All covetousness is spiritual. Any so-called material thing that you want is merely a symbol: you want it not for itself, but because it will content your spirit for the moment."

We can't put too fine a point on how deadly a covetous attitude is in life. At the heart of covetousness is a lack of gratitude for what we already have. David already had multiple wives and concubines, and, given that he was the king of Israel and head and shoulders above every other man of his time, we can assume that he had his pick among all the women on the planet. Apparently, the women he already had weren't enough. Chinese philosopher Laozi rightly observed, "Covetousness is the greatest misfortune. One who does not know what is enough will never have enough." David, like all of us, wasn't content with what he had. His lack of contentment made him ravenous to have more, which didn't satisfy him either.

Overcoming a Covetous Attitude

We all covet having something or someone. We all struggle to some degree with the green-eyed monster of envying what others have that we don't. Here are some tips for how to overcome being covetous.

Acknowledge That What You Covet is an Idol in Your Life. There is a difference between *wanting* something that we would be *disappointed* if we didn't get and *coveting* something that we would be *devastated* if we didn't ever have. We can know something has become an idol when we base our happiness and well-being on having it. Write down the things you covet in life, that, were you not to get them, you would be completely miserable and unhappy.

Sacrificially Give in the Areas Where You Covet. If you covet being loved, turn this around by loving others. If you covet wealth, give more of your money away. If you covet having a high position at work, help others attain it. Play the "Opposite Game" with yourself and sacrificially give in the very areas you covet having more.

Rejoice with Those Who Have What You Covet. If you covet a nicer home, rejoice with those who have a nicer home than you. If you covet having the freedom to travel more, rejoice with those who get to travel all over the world. If you covet your neighbor's spouse, rejoice with him or her that they have found such an awesome person. If you covet how your friend's kids turned out, rejoice with them that their kids turned out so well. Celebrate with others that life has blessed them in such wonderful ways.

Count Your Many Blessings. I grew up singing a song in church along these lines, and it has always stuck with me. The song went, "Count your blessings, name them one by one, count your blessings, see what God has done!" If you have a problem coveting what others have, count your many blessings each day when it comes to what you already have. Even if you don't have as nice a home, car, clothes, travel options, income, or position of influence as others do, count your blessings that you have a home, car, clothes, get to travel (even if it is just to the grocery store), income, a job, or the like. We are more blessed than we realize and need to take our eyes off of how much more blessed others might be.

Pay More Attention to the Person Than You Do to What They Have That You Covet. Far too often, we pay attention to what people have rather than the person who has it. We lose sight of the fact that they are a human being who finds life difficult and painful just like we do. People having what we want doesn't mean their life is any better or easier than ours. We need to stop seeing people as "wealthy," "powerful," "influential," or "famous" and see them as fellow struggling human beings who are having just as hard a time making their way through life as we do. Don't lose sight of the *human being* in front of you by only focusing on all they have.

Coveting what others have damages your soul and keeps you from interacting with others in a loving and empathic manner. I hope these tips for overcoming a covetous attitude were helpful to you.

Some Final Thoughts

In the film *Wall Street,* legendary Wall Street investor Gordon Gekko says in an iconic speech to company shareholders, "The point is, ladies and gentleman, that greed, for the lack of a better word, is good. Greed is right, greed works. Greed clarifies, cuts through, and captures the essence of the evolutionary spirit. Greed, in all of its forms; greed for life, for money, for love, knowledge has marked the upward surge of mankind." Even though Gordon Gekko is a fictional character, he represents a lot of people who go out into the world each day greedily in pursuit of wealth, power, and sex.

I disagree with Gordon Gekko. Greed is not good. Greed is always a reflection of covetousness. Greed is a sign you have taken something good (in Gekko's case, money) and turned it in to an idol, an ultimate source of well-being and happiness in life. For Gordon Gekko, the idol in question was wealth. In the movie, Gekko came tumbling down off his high horse because he coveted wealth so much that he broke the law to attain more of it.

Irish playwright Isaac Bickerstaffe once said, "But if I'm content with a little, enough is as good as a feast." He's right. If we could challenge ourselves to be content with the fundamental basics in life—food, clothing, shelter, relationships, meaningful work—anything beyond that would truly be a feast.

Is your life caught up in coveting what you don't have, or do you feel like what you already have is "as good as a feast"? Are you coveting that Stingray bike or thankful for the one you already have? Are you coveting your boss's job or thankful for the one you have? Are you coveting your neighbor's spouse, home, car, vacations, success, or bank account or thankful for all the versions of those things you have?

We could all work on being content with little so that enough would feel like a feast. Given that a lot of the things we covet never show up around the Christmas tree, it's not a bad idea. The challenge of being more content is a hard one in our country because so many of us already have so much. When you already have a lot but constantly look around to see if others have more, it makes it pretty hard to be content with little. Nevertheless, let's give Isaac Bickerstaffe's challenge a try and work on being content with a little.

Think About It

1. When you were growing up, what did you covet?

2. As an adult, what are some of the people, places, and things you find yourself coveting now?

3. Do you ever find yourself being content with little such that enough is as much as a feast?

Chapter 9

Settling for Less: A Complacent Attitude

The tragedy of life is not found in failure but in complacency. Not in doing too much but in doing too little. Not in living above your means, but below your capacity. It's not failure but aiming too low, that is life's greatest tragedy.

—Benjamin E. Mays

I know your deeds, that you are neither cold nor hot.
I wish you were either one or the other.

—Revelation 3:15

I'm fairly cynical (admittedly, not a good attitude) about a lot of the personal empowerment stuff that's out there. I think it wrongly tries to pump us up into thinking we need to "awaken the giant within" and tap our "unlimited power." To my way of thinking, we need to awaken the finite human being within and use what little personal power we have in life more effectively if we want to experience healthy and successful lives. That being said, I appreciate what the personal empowerment movement is trying to do—get us to quit being complacent and bring a lot more "juice" to our efforts to live life fully.

Not to put it too bluntly, but far too many of us are complacent when it comes to developing ourselves. It's one reason why I don't take court-ordered cases—if a judge has to order someone to come to counseling to work on their issues, I'm probably not going to be able to get anywhere with them.

Basketball coach Don Meyer once said, "Complacency is the forerunner of mediocrity. You can never work too hard on attitudes, effort and technique." He ought to know. At one point in his career, Meyer held the record for most wins in college basketball history. A complacent attitude will ensure that your life will be mediocre at best.

I grew up an Air Force brat. One of the things I admire most about the military is their emphasis on training soldiers to overcome their complacency and "be all that you can be." My parents raised my brothers and me that way, and that is how Holly and I tried to raise our own three kids. We simply weren't going to let them be lazy or complacent in how they went through life, at least not on our watch.

Let me give you one of the quintessential examples of a military man who was known for being all that he could be and pushing his troops to be the same. He left an indelible mark on the military and was one of the key reasons the allies won World War II. His aversion to complacency brought out the best in everyone around him, and, while he was often criticized for the way he did things, he led soldiers to victories that were seemingly impossible. We would be wise to model our lives after someone like this, a person who was anything but complacent in how he helped lead our country in one of its finest moments.

Old Blood and Guts

He was born November 11, 1885, in a family that had an extensive military background. He graduated from the US Military Academy at West Point and was skilled enough in the modern pentathlon that he competed in the 1912 Summer Olympics. He first saw combat during the Pancho Villa Expedition in 1916 and was part of the first military action using armored vehicles. He saw action in World War I, commanding a tank school in France before being wounded. He was a central figure in developing the Army's armored warfare doctrine and rose through the ranks rapidly. By the time America entered into World War II, he commanded the 2nd Armored Division. He quickly established himself as an effective commander. He commanded the 7th Army during the Allied invasion of Sicily, the 3rd Army that rapidly drove across France, and was named the military governor of Bavaria after the war ended.

He was also known for being arrogant, driven, and foul-mouthed. He got himself in trouble on numerous occasions, once for slapping two

shell-shocked soldiers under his command. Some of the commanding of-
ficers over him in World War II didn't particularly like his bombastic style
of leadership but appreciated the things he was able to accomplish on the
battlefield. The German High Command had a great deal of respect for
his leadership abilities and never wanted to go up against his troops. He
got his nickname, "Old Blood and Guts," because he told his troops that's
what they were going to be up to their neck in during battle. Because he
pushed his men so hard in battle, a common quip among his troops was,
"Yeah, our blood, his guts."

George Smith Patton became an American folk hero because of his
style and great accomplishments. His status as a military hero was solidi-
fied in the movie *Patton,* which won seven Academy Awards, including
Best Picture, Best Director, and Best Actor for George C. Scott. I bring
all this up to talk about a scene in the movie that drives home just how
deadly a complacent attitude can be for any of us when we are out on the
battlefield of life.

The US Army had just gotten its fanny kicked by German General Erwin Rommel at the Battle of Kasserine Pass in North Africa, and
General George Patton was called in to restore order and discipline. The
scene in the movie *Patton* I'm reminded of is when he arrives at Army
headquarters in North Africa and finds everyone laying around. Patton
comes across a soldier who is half-asleep and asks, "What were you doing
down there?" The soldier replies, "Trying to get some sleep, sir." The hard-
charging general responds, "Well . . . get back down there, son. You're the
only son of a bitch here who knows what he is trying to do." Patton patted
this soldier on the back for at least not being complacent about trying to
get some sleep. Patton proceeded to instill discipline and hard work in
the troops and was able to drive Rommel out of North Africa. He was
rewarded for doing so by being given the 7th Army and allowed to invade
Sicily, which he did successfully.

The famous speech at the opening of *Patton* was based on an actual
speech Patton gave to the the 3rd Army prior to the Allied invasion of
France. The movie cleaned Patton's speech up quite a bit—it is profanity
laced and unflinching in its description of what he challenged American
troops to do to the German Army. The thing that stood out to me about his
speech are the places where he says things like, "I don't want any messages
saying 'I'm holding my position.' We're not holding a (expletive) thing . . .
We're advancing constantly . . . Our plan of operation is to advance and

keep on advancing . . . There will be some complaints that we're pushing our people too hard. I don't give a damn about such complaints. I believe that an ounce of sweat will save a gallon of blood. The harder we push, the more Germans we kill. The more Germans we kill, the fewer of our men will be killed . . . My men don't surrender. I don't want to hear of any soldier under my command being captured unless he is hit. Even if you are hit, you can still fight . . ."

Perhaps the main reason Patton was such an effective leader was the fact that he didn't have a complacent bone in his body. "Our plan of operation is to advance and keep on advancing." Yikes. No wonder Patton had the nickname "Old Blood and Guts." He knew that complacency had gotten the US Army defeated in North Africa, and he wasn't about to ever let it happen again.

If we can shift phrasing for a minute, we're talking here about the human bent toward laziness, cutting corners when it comes to the level of effort we need in order to be excellent at our endeavors in life. Far too many of us are lazy when it comes to being physically fit, managing finances properly, working on our marriages, raising our kids properly, developing stronger friendships, and fostering our spiritual growth. This is the pot calling the kettle black because I have seen throughout my own life a tendency to not be hardworking enough when it comes to these crucial areas of life. Consequently, I have been too complacent about fitness, finances, marriage, kids, friendships, and spiritual growth than I should have been. As Benjamin Mays put it above, I have "lived below [my] capacity."

We can all do better than that, me included. We aren't going to win very many battles in life if we don't have a Pattonesque "We're advancing constantly" attitude when it comes to the level of effort we need to put into the important things in life.

Overcoming a Complacent Attitude

If you find yourself throwing a half-baked effort at important areas of life, you might want to try the following.

Focus on a Specific Area Where You Want to Grow and Write Down How You Want to Improve and What It Would Take to Do It. What vision to you have for a given area of your life in terms of how you would like to see yourself grow and what would you have to do to be victorious? Be realistic and specific. Grandiose and unfocused goals don't work. Get your target in focus and specifically spell out the steps you have to take to achieve it.

Get an Accountability Partner. Far too often, we have a vision for how we would like to grow or improve but we do it Lone Ranger style. But even the Lone Ranger had Tonto. Find a person who is a little bit ahead of you in the area you want to grow in and ask them to meet with you to hold you accountable for implementing your strategy.

Reward Yourself When You Get Off Your Bottom. When you hold your own feet to the fire and do what you need to do in an effort to improve, properly reward yourself. I say properly because if you go and do a workout to lose weight you don't want to reward yourself with a cheeseburger, fries, and shake. When you do what you are supposed to do in moving toward achieving your goals, find some healthy way to pat yourself on the back. Behavior that is reinforced is likely to continue.

Don't Allow Setbacks to Defeat You. When you get thrown from the horse, don't go back to being lazy about changing who you are. *Never quit!* Even if you take fifty steps back, get up, dust yourself off, get back up on the horse, and try again. Also, make sure you are honest with your accountability partner about what happened so that he or she can lovingly and firmly challenge you to keep advancing.

Be an Accountability Partner for Someone Else. There is nothing more motivating to stay the course in growing in your own life than holding someone else accountable for doing the same. Few of us like to be hypocrites. So, in your efforts to get your act together, be the accountability partner for someone trying to get their act together.

Some Final Thoughts

There are many reasons I love the movie *Rocky*. I'm a sucker for a good rags-to-riches story. What I love the most about Rocky is his transformation from a complacent, lazy club fighter to a hardworking, dedicated world-class fighter who becomes an inspiration to the people in Philadelphia, and, ultimately, around the world.

Rocky went from being an out-of-shape neighborhood thug collecting gambling debts for a local bookmaker to, as his trainer, Mickey, put it, a fighter who "spits lightning and craps thunder." Once Rocky was given the dauting task of fighting the world heavyweight boxing champion, Apollo Creed, he reached deep down inside his soul, found his capacity to be great lurking there, and completely turned his life around.

Did Rocky "awaken the giant within" or discover that he had "unlimited power"? Depends on who you ask. If you ask most motivational speakers, the answer is yes. If you ask me, the answer is no. I think what he did was find the spark of motivation inside his soul, rediscover the power that was in him to make his life more than he had allowed it to be, and become an iconic role model for the rest us.

Which version of Rocky are you? Are you the Rocky who is out of shape, barely getting by, taking on fights that don't bring out the best in you, and feeling satisfied with your win-loss record against other club fighters? Or, are you the Rocky that took on a seemingly impossible task, allowed it to bring out of you the full measure of what you have to offer the world, and went fifteen rounds with the best that life could throw at you?

Complacency is a killer. It will keep you from making your life all that it could be. You've got a lot more inside of you than you realize. If you will get off the mat and put more effort into maximizing your potential, you might be surprised how far you can go in life.

Think About It

1. In what areas of your life are you lazy and complacent? What has been the cost of being that way?

2. Where in your life have you been hardworking and disciplined? How have you benefitted from being that way?

3. What one area of life are you currently being complacent about and what can you do to raise the bar, work harder, and bring out your best?

Chapter 10

How Do I Stack Up? A Comparing Attitude

Comparison is an act of violence against the self.

—Iyanla Vanzant

Each one should test their own actions. Then they can take pride in
themselves alone, without comparing themselves to someone else.

—Galatians 6:4

Nike got roundly criticized for an ad campaign during the 1996
Olympics that said, "You don't win silver, you lose gold." Think about
that for a minute. You have the premier athletic shoe company in the world
telling competitors who are *the second best in the world* they actually lost.
Can you imagine being the second best at something in a world of billions
of people and being told that you are a loser? What an incredibly insulting
and dismissive thing to say.

Yet, this is the attitude some people have as they go through life, even
teaching it to their kids. I saw a teenager in a mall once who had a t-shirt
that read, "Second place is the first loser." I sat there thinking how sad it is
for kids to be raised in a world where, like the Nike ad, they are told that unless they are number one, they might as well believe they finished last. How
many parents, teachers, and coaches have trotted out this line of nonsense
in a misguided effort to motivate kids to reach their full potential?

I used to have this attitude myself every summer when my brothers
and I would congregate in San Diego with our families. We stupidly timed

the trip to coincide with a half-marathon in the city and ran it together. I say "stupidly" because I really didn't do anything to train for the race—I just kind of showed up and decided in the name of brotherhood, bonding, and Southern California sunshine to run 13.1 miles without having put in sufficient effort to prepare. Stupid.

That's not the worst part. The worst part is that when I was out on the race course, I kept comparing myself with the other runners. This was especially problematic when we entered a park where we could see all the runners ahead of us coming out of the park. And, they weren't just a little ahead of us, they were a mile or so ahead of us. It was at that point in the race that I felt like cutting across the divide to join them or turning around and mocking the three people behind me.

Think about that. I haven't trained for a rather lengthy race and yet I'm looking all around me, upset with the people who are ahead of me (who actually trained) and looking down my nose at the people who are behind me (who probably weren't even officially entered in the race and didn't train at all). What am I doing comparing myself to these people? What did their ability to run faster or slower have to do with me? Every runner had their own body, put in a certain amount of preparation, and was motivated in different ways and for different reasons. What possessed me to compare myself to them?

The world we live in seems to have an obsession with being number one. This obsession has, at times, led to sports fans to get into it with each, even to the point of inflicting bodily harm and causing death. Let's call it what it is: comparison taken to craziness.

Comparison Taken Much Too Far

I'm a huge fan of college football, especially when it comes to my beloved Texas Longhorns. I have been a Longhorn fan since 1969. Yep, I've been a fan for more than half a century. To say I've seen my share of highs and lows as a Texas fan would be an understatement. I've experienced the lows of losing seasons and the highs of a national championship in 2005 when the Longhorns beat what was considered to be one of the greatest college football teams of all time, the University of Southern California Trojans. I've watched the replay of that game approximately 3,406 times and savored each second of our highest moment in college football history.

Our archrival throughout the years was the Texas A&M Aggies. We used to be in the same conference, and the Texas–Texas A&M game was long considered one of the greatest rivalries in college football. It didn't matter who had the best record going into the game, each contest was fiercely fought and if you won that game it made your whole season. The first game was played in 1894 and the last game in 2001. Just in case you were wondering, my Longhorns lead the series with 76 wins, 37 losses, and 5 ties.

The Longhorns and Aggies have played a lot of pranks on each other over the years, even though, behind it all, we have a great deal of respect for each other. The most famous prank of all took place in 1916. Texas won the Thanksgiving game that year, 21–7, and thought about branding their longhorn steer mascot, Bevo, with the score. Before they could, some Aggie pranksters tracked Bevo down and branded him with the score of the 1915 game, which Texas A&M won 13–0. The legend goes that Texas students took some branding equipment and turned 13–0 into "BEVO" and that is how our mascot got his name, but that actually isn't true. Because it was too expensive to keep Bevo fed and cared for during World War I, Texas ended up barbecuing him for a sports banquet in 1920, invited some Aggies to attend, and presented them with the hide that still had 13–0 on it.

Longhorn fans returned the favor in 1993. They kidnapped A&M's mascot, a purebred Rough Collie named Reveille VI, before the Aggies played Notre Dame in the Cotton Bowl. A group of Texas students called the "Rustlers" demanded a ransom—"A&M had to publicly announce that Reveille had been stolen and state that UT was superior to A&M." Since Reveille was valued at more than $750, the abduction was a third-degree felony punishable by two to ten years in prison and a fine up to $10,000. So, the Rustlers, being the intelligent college students they were, tied Reveille up to a sign post near Lake Travis in Austin, left him there, and the Aggies got their precious dog back.

This kind of competitive spirit among college football rivals is a lot of fun when not taken too far. No one gets hurt, everyone involved gets to make the point that they think the other school stinks, and we have a good laugh about it. What seems to be happening more often in sports is when things turn violent among overly competitive fans.

It was disturbing to read that after Alabama played LSU in Baton Rouge in 2018, a game the Crimson Tide won, an Alabama fan was brutally beaten to death by two LSU fans in a bar fight. The two men accused of committing the crime were charged with manslaughter. How insane that a human being would die because fans from two different schools got into it with each other about the outcome of a college football game.

This reminds me of other notorious events where an unhealthy competitive attitude led to people doing some horrible things—Nancy Kerrigan being kneecapped in an assault planned by her chief competitor's husband, Lance Armstrong using performance-enhancing drugs to win seven Tour de France titles, the New England Patriots using under-inflated footballs because they were easier to throw and catch . . . the list goes on and on. Competition can bring out the very best in us, but it can also bring out the very worst.

If we are going to compare ourselves in life, let's compare ourselves with ourselves. Let's compete with ourselves to bring out our personal best in an effort to fully steward the talents and abilities we have been given. Betty Jamie Chung got it right when she said, "Comparison with myself brings improvement, comparison with others brings discontent." Theodore Roosevelt insightfully noted, "Comparison is the thief of joy." Finally, Eugenia Herlihy wisely observed, "Comparison is the most poisonous element in the human heart because it destroys ingenuity and robs peace and joy."

Overcoming a Comparing Attitude

There are dozens of reasons why comparing yourself to others is "the thief of joy" and destructive to your life. Here are some tips for how to resist the unhealthy impulse to compare who you are, what you have, or what you have accomplished to others.

Focus on Your Strengths. Try to avoid looking at other people's strengths and just zero in on your own. If you are going to look at where you are deficient in some way that you don't like, try to think about it from the perspective of how you can improve so you can turn a weakness into a strength.

Remind Yourself That Everyone is Unique. One of the main reasons comparing yourself with others is unhealthy is that everyone is unique. You can't truly compare any human being with another because every human being is a complex, nuanced, "stand-alone" individual who has been gifted and equipped in different ways at different levels. Think about yourself from the perspective of taking what *you* have been given and trying to improve on it.

Acknowledge That Comparing Yourself with Others is Always Unfair. Because we come equipped with different talents and abilities and have different life experiences along the way, comparing yourself with others is inherently unfair. To use an analogy, why would you compare yourself with another athlete who was born with greater talent and received better instruction and training along the way? Why would you compare yourself with someone born with lesser talent who got inadequate instruction and training along the way?

Admit There is No End to Comparing and It is a Waste of Time. Remind yourself that there will always be people to compare yourself to and that it is a total waste of your time. No matter how old you get or what level of success you attain, there will always be people who did better and who did worse than you. Don't waste your time and energy doing something that doesn't leave you better off.

Realize that Comparing Yourself with Others Only Leads to Resentment and Bitterness. If you are prone to compare yourself with others who are better than you in some way or have more than you, you inevitably end up bitter. You walk around feeling cheated and short-changed by life (or God) and resentful for coming out on the short end of the stick. Try to be thankful for the success your abilities, talents, and hard work helped you achieve.

Comparing yourself with others is a useless and destructive waste of time. May I, as someone who struggles with this as much as you, encourage all of us to stop comparing ourselves with others and focus on being the best version of ourselves we can be? Let's compete with ourselves to fully steward the gifts and abilities we have been given and quit worrying about how we compare to others.

Some Final Thoughts

I'm sure you can tell by now that I am a big movie fan. One of my all-time favorites is *Hoosiers*. The film was loosely based on the Milan High School basketball team in Indiana that won the 1954 state championship against a much larger school. *Hoosiers* is about a small Indiana town that hires Norman Dale, a former college coach, to coach their high school basketball team. I say "former college coach" because Dale had been kicked out of college basketball for striking one of his players.

If you know anything about Indiana, you know that basketball is a religion in the state, similar to how football is a religion in Texas. Even though the town is so small that there are only seven players on the team, none of whom have been properly taught to play the game of basketball, it isn't long before the townspeople are upset with Coach Dale because of his seemingly odd coaching methods and the fact that the team doesn't start off the season playing very well. They unsuccessfully try to have him fired.

Coach Dale sticks to his guns because he is incredibly talented when it comes to how to teach kids to play basketball. And, with the town's best player joining the team, they begin to play "lights out." They play so well they end up making it through the playoffs to the championship game by beating teams from schools that had much larger enrollments. Prior to their semifinal tournament game, Coach Dale gives what is considered one of the best sports speeches in movie history. Here's what he told his players:

> There's a tradition in tournament play to not talk about the next step until you've climbed the one in front of you. I'm sure going to the state finals is beyond your wildest dreams, so let's just keep it right there. Forget about the crowds, the size of the school, their fancy uniforms, and remember what got you here. Focus on the fundamentals that we've gone over time and time again, and, most important, don't get caught up in thinking about winning or losing this game. If you put your effort and concentration into playing to your potential, to be the best that you can be, I don't care what the scoreboard says at the end of the game, in my book, we're going to be winners! Okay?

That's getting it right. Life is a competition, and we need to get in the game. But, let's stop competing with others as if everything is a zero-sum game with only winners and losers. When we compete against others, let's make the real competition with ourselves. Let's "forget about the crowds, the size of the school, their fancy uniforms." Let's "focus on the fundamentals," not "get caught up in thinking about winning or losing this game," "put your effort and concentration into playing to your potential," and "be the best that you can be." If we do that, it doesn't matter what the scoreboard reads, we're going to be winners. Okay?

Think About It

1. What areas of life do you find that you compare yourself with others? How does doing so leave you feeling?

2. What would it be like to compare yourself only with yourself and work hard on bringing out the best from your God-given talents and abilities?

3. Given your tendency to compare, has it been hard to enjoy other people's success or encourage those less successful?

Chapter 11

I'm God's Gift to the Planet:
A Conceited Attitude

I'm not conceited. Conceit is a fault and I have no faults.

—David Lee Roth

Do you see a person who is wise in their own eyes?
There is more hope for a fool than for them.

—Proverbs 26:12

I'm fascinated by how people handle being gifted and talented. These people often fall into one of two main camps: those who understand their talents and abilities are not their own and humbly share them while they're here, and those who think they are the source of their gifts and abilities and act like they are doing the world a favor to share them with us. All of us have some degree of the latter in us, a conceited attitude that gets in the way of appreciating the skills and abilities we have been given and using them for the right reasons.

You may think I've already covered being conceited in the chapter on having a cocky attitude. I may be splitting semantic hairs here, but to me being cocky and being conceited are two very different things. Being cocky means that you are *overly* confident about being able to perform or achieve at a high level. Being conceited means that you think way too highly of yourself for being talented. Sure, these are bedfellows to some degree, but they are different mindsets that often come together to make people truly insufferable. Put cockiness together with conceit and you have a human being who is going to stomp around the planet thinking they are blessing our socks off that we get to enjoy their awesomeness.

Let me drive all this home by comparing two incredibly talented people who seem to have much different attitudes about being gifted.

Wooden Versus West

John Wooden is considered the greatest college basketball coach of all time. While he was the coach of the UCLA Bruins, his teams won *ten* national championships in a *twelve-year period*. At one point, Wooden's teams won *seven national titles in a row*. A great college basketball player in his own right, he was named a basketball All-American three times. As a coach, Wooden was named the national coach of the year a record seven times. In 1972, he shared *Sport Illustrated*'s Sportsman of the Year award with Billie Jean King. In 2009 was named *Sporting News'* "Greatest Coach of All Time," and the college basketball player-of-the-year award bears his name. Wooden is the first and only person to be enshrined into the Basketball Hall of Fame as both a player (1960) and a coach (1973).

You would think that all of that success would go to John Wooden's head and that he might start to think he was God's gift to college basketball. Think again. Wooden is an oft-quoted man, but my favorite quote of his is this one: "Talent is God-given. Be humble. Fame is man-given. Be grateful. Conceit is self-given. Be careful." Think about that. Here is a man who had unparalleled success in his area of expertise, and he attributes his talent to God, his fame to man, and warns people against becoming conceited about either. John Wooden wasn't conceited because he knew his talent came from God and that earthly fame was just icing on the cake.

Kanye West is an American singer, songwriter, record producer, fashion designer, and business entrepreneur. He is one of the most awarded music artists of all time, having won twenty-one Grammy Awards. West has sold over 135 million records worldwide, a number of his albums have been included in *Rolling Stone*'s "500 Greatest Albums of All Time," and *Time* Magazine named him one of the "100 Most Influential People" in 2005 and 2015. He was the first non-athlete to be given a shoe deal by Nike, is one of the most critically-acclaimed artists of the twenty-first century, all of his studio albums have gone platinum (one million or more in sales), and holds the record for the most albums to debut at number one on the *Billboard* 200.

You would think all this success would go to Kanye West's head and that he might start to think he was God's gift to music and fashion design. You'd be right. Kayne West said he will go down in history as "the voice of this generation," stormed out of an awards show when he didn't win "Best New Artist," saying "I felt like I was definitely robbed . . . I was the best new artist of the year," went on to the stage at the 2006 MTV Europe Music Awards when he didn't win "Best Video" and argued that he should have won, proclaimed that "God has chosen me to be the voice and the connector" here on earth, and, most infamously, went up on stage and grabbed the microphone from Taylor Swift when she won Best Female Video at the 2009 MTV Music Video Awards, boasting that the video he produced for Beyoncé "was one of the best videos of all time" and should have won the award.

Lest you think I am being insensitive to West's mental health issues, I'm not. No one seems to be sure what mental health problems he struggles with; some have suggested he suffers from bipolar disorder, experienced nervous breakdowns and paranoid delusions, and has had moments of suicidal ideation. I hope it goes without saying that as a psychologist I have great empathy for anyone who struggles with serious mental health issues. That being said, there are a lot of people who have serious psychological problems who don't struggle with a conceited attitude, and I sometimes wonder if a conceited attitude is what leads *some* people to have significant mental health issues.

Now, let's compare John Wooden to Kayne West. Both are extremely talented, have experienced tremendous fame, achieved a great deal of success, and won a lot of awards. But, look at how different their reaction has been. John Wooden saw talent as God-given and something to be humble about, fame as man-given and something to be grateful for, and conceit as self-given and something to be careful about. Kanye West also sees talent as God-given but seems to see fame as something he is entitled to and appears oblivious to just how conceited he is about all the success that has come his way.

All this reminds me of a statement by Louisa May Alcott, author of *Little Women*: "You may have a good many gifts and virtues, but there is no need of parading them, for conceit spoils the finest genius. There is not much danger that real talent or goodness will be overlooked long, and the great charm of all power is modesty." It also reminds of a statement in Proverbs, "Let someone else praise you, and not your own mouth; an outsider, and not your own lips" (27:2). Words to the wise, wouldn't you agree?

John Wooden, not Kayne West, has it right. Talent is God-given and we are to be humble about whatever level of it we have. Fame is man-given and something we are to be grateful for. Conceit is self-given and something to be *very* careful about. Whatever talent we have and whatever fame we enjoy, we are not to ever conceitedly act like either is about us.

Overcoming a Conceited Attitude

Yes, I know, it's hard not to be conceited when you're awesome. Nevertheless, here are some tips for how to overcome being conceited about what your good at and what level of earthly adoration it has led to.

Walk Inside Other's Shoes and Try to See Life Through Their Eyes. It's pretty hard to think "you're all that" when you have compassion about how hard some people struggle in life and how much dignity they exhibit in the face of it. If we have an overly high opinion of ourselves, we would do well to pay attention how well some of the lowly and downtrodden handle their struggles and use them as inspiration for the attitude we need to have in life.

Laugh at Yourself. If you're conceited, you probably lost your sense of humor along the way, especially when it comes to just how human and mistake-prone you are. Conceitedness has a way of keeping you from laughing at your foibles and peccadillos. Try to get your sense of humor back and laugh (non-derisively) at just how human you are.

Try to Stop Being Right. Conceitedness often leads us to trying to prove we're the sharpest knife in the drawer. We're not, and we are only disrespecting others when we need to prove we're right and they're wrong. Let's stop trying to prove we're right, humbly share our opinion, and remain open-minded to what we might learn from others.

Let Others Speak and Listen Better. Why did God give us two ears and one mouth? Because he wants us to listen more than we speak. When we have an overly high opinion of ourselves, we think people should listen to us rather than us to them. Try doing this: listen for two minutes for every one minute you speak. You'll be amazed how much you might learn.

Do Things That Humble You. Let others go first in line, be the center of attention, and receive praise. Do some version of "washing other's feet," things that would be humbling to do and help knock some of the conceitedness out of you. If you really want to deal with being conceited, each time you encounter someone, ask them "What can I do to serve you today?" That will keep you humble.

An overly high opinion of yourself, just like an overly low opinion of yourself, is a hard thing to change. Nevertheless, these are some ways you can properly eat some humble pie and see yourself more accurately over time. You're not God's gift to the planet, but you do have some important and valuable things to offer, even if it's just your time and attention.

Some Final Thoughts

Conceit is an ugly thing. Whenever I think about being conceited, I think about Carly Simon's song "You're So Vain." The song is about someone Simon had a relationship with who was a conceited, narcissistic kind of guy. For you music trivia buffs, debate raged for years about who Simon was referring to, and she finally revealed that certain lyrics in the song are about Hollywood lothario Warren Beatty. The point of the song was that Beatty was conceited, something he was known for in Hollywood, even to the point that Simon says, "I'll bet you think this song is about you." Never be conceited toward a talented singer/songwriter—it might come back to bite you.

Harry Emerson Fosdick said, "A person wrapped up in himself makes a small package." If you struggle with being conceited, try to see life through other people's eyes, laugh at your own humanness, listen more than you talk, and humbly serve others. Do yourself a favor and come down off your high horse as soon as possible. Join the human race and accept the fact that you're as finite and fallen as the rest of us. You don't want a song written about you, do you?

Think About It

1. What talents, abilities or achievements in the past have you been conceited about?

2. What in the here and now have you accomplished that you have been conceited about?

3. How do you feel when you hear someone else tooting their own horn about the success they've achieved or the talents and abilities they have?

Chapter 12

Flat-Out Mean and Hateful:
A Caustic Attitude

The satirist who writes nothing but satire should write but little—or it will seem that his satire springs rather from his own caustic nature than from the sins of the world in which he lives.

—Anthony Trollope

Anyone who claims to be in the light but hates
a brother or sister is still in darkness.

—1 John 3:15

When you think of the word *caustic*, I want you to think *corrosive*. Let's take a quick look at defining both words.

The *Cambridge Dictionary* says a "caustic remark or way of speaking is hurtful, critical, or intentionally unkind." Vocabulary.com says "The word *corrosive* comes from the Latin word, *corrodere*, meaning 'to gnaw away.'" *Rodere*, to gnaw, is the same root word for *rodent*, so you can think about the word *corrosive* as something that gnaws through things like a rodent. The adjective *corrosive* is also used to describe something that is bitingly or spitefully sarcastic. When referring to a chemical, corrosive means "causing damage to metal or other materials through a chemical process." Let me give you an example from my own life about just how corrosive chemicals can be.

I may have already mentioned that I'm a perfectionistic, something that extends to pretty much every area of my life. When it comes to my home, for example, everything has to be organized, polished, shined, cleaned, and shipshape. One day I got the bright idea to thoroughly clean my garage floor of all the oil stains. So, I trotted down to the local hardware store, asked the experts what to do, and they suggested I buy some muriatic acid and acid-wash the garage floor. They warned me to dilute the muriatic acid with water, advice I proceeded to completely ignore.

Once I got back home, I poured the muriatic acid directly on the garage floor, figuring that doing so would *deeply* remove all the oil stains. Keep in mind that I'm in my garage and only the garage door is open. No sooner had I poured the acid on the floor than I almost died from asphyxiation from the fumes and compounded all that by splashing acid directly on my legs. I ran out of the garage like my hair was on fire, hoping I hadn't permanently damaged my lungs and wouldn't need to be on a respirator the rest of my life. I'm thankful none of my neighbors saw this because I'm sure they would have called EMS and I would have had a huge medical bill to pay for on top of all my idiocy.

I bring this up to say that I experienced firsthand just how corrosive certain chemicals are and just how deadly they can be to our physical selves. Now, let me circle back around to interpersonal relationships. Some of us have a caustic attitude when it comes to how we talk to or about other people. Some of us spew corrosive words at others, more often than not to make ourselves look better, and we don't seem to care that much about how damaging these words are to the soul of another.

In the next section, I'm going to focus on a person in the entertainment world who has come to epitomize a caustic attitude toward those *in his own industry*, and he has justifiably received a lot of negative blowback for it.

Caustic Host of the Year

It happened at the seventy-seventh Golden Globe Awards in 2020. The culprit was the one hosting the awards, Ricky Gervais. This was his fifth time hosting the Golden Globes, an awards show put on by the Hollywood Foreign Press Association to honor excellence in television and film, and Gervais took the gloves completely off that evening. It shocked the Hollywood glitterati in attendance, something that is not all that easy to do.

Rather than tell you that Gervais delivered one of the most caustic opening monologues of all time at an awards show, I'm just going to let you read what he said so you can decide for yourself. For your protection, I removed a paragraph from the monologue that was especially disgusting. Strap on your seatbelt.

> Hello and welcome to the seventy-seventh annual Golden Globe Awards, live from the Beverly Hilton Hotel here in Los Angeles. I'm Ricky Gervais, thank you.
>
> You'll be pleased to know this is the last time I'm hosting these awards, so I don't care anymore. I'm joking. I never did. NBC clearly doesn't care either—fifth time. I mean, Kevin Hart was fired from the Oscars for some offensive tweets—hello?
>
> Lucky for me, the Hollywood Foreign Press can barely speak English and they've no idea what Twitter is, so I got offered this gig by fax. Let's go out with a bang, let's have a laugh at your expense. Remember, they're just jokes. We're all gonna die soon and there's no sequel, so remember that.
>
> But you all look lovely all dolled up. You came here in your limos. I came here in a limo tonight and the license plate was made by Felicity Huffman. No, shush. It's her daughter I feel sorry for. OK? That must be the most embarrassing thing that's ever happened to her. And her dad was in *Wild Hogs*.
>
> Lots of big celebrities here tonight. Legends. Icons. This table alone—Al Pacino, Robert DeNiro . . . Baby Yoda. Oh, that's Joe Pesci, sorry. I love you man. Don't have me whacked. But tonight isn't just about the people in front of the camera. In this room are some of the most important TV and film executives in the world. People from every background. They all have one thing in common: They're all terrified of Ronan Farrow. He's coming for ya. Talking of all you perverts, it was a big year for pedophile movies. *Surviving R. Kelly, Leaving Neverland, Two Popes*. Shut up. Shut up. I don't care. I don't care.
>
> Many talented people of color were snubbed in major categories. Unfortunately, there's nothing we can do about that. Hollywood Foreign Press are all very racist. Fifth time. So, we were going to do an In Memoriam this year, but when I saw the list of people who died, it wasn't diverse enough. No, it was mostly white people and I thought, nah, not on my watch. Maybe next year. Let's see what happens.
>
> No one cares about movies anymore. No one goes to cinema, no one really watches network TV. Everyone is watching Netflix. This show should just be me coming out, going, "Well done,

Netflix. You win everything. Good night." But no, we got to drag it out for three hours. You could binge-watch the entire first season of *Afterlife* instead of watching this show. That's a show about a man who wants to kill himself cause his wife dies of cancer and it's still more fun than this. Spoiler alert, season two is on the way so in the end he obviously didn't kill himself. Just like Jeffrey Epstein. Shut up. I know he's your friend but I don't care.

Seriously, most films are awful. Lazy. Remakes, sequels. I've heard a rumor there might be a sequel to *Sophie's Choice*. I mean, that would just be Meryl just going, "Well, it's gotta be this one then." All the best actors have jumped to Netflix, HBO. And the actors who just do Hollywood movies now do fantasy-adventure nonsense. They wear masks and capes and really tight costumes. Their job isn't acting anymore. It's going to the gym twice a day and taking steroids, really. Have we got an award for most ripped junky? No point, we'd know who'd win that.

Martin Scorsese made the news for his controversial comments about the Marvel franchise. He said they're not real cinema and they remind him about theme parks. I agree. Although I don't know what he's doing hanging around theme parks. He's not big enough to go on the rides. He's tiny. *The Irishman* was amazing. It was amazing. It was great. Long, but amazing. It wasn't the only epic movie. *Once Upon a Time in Hollywood*, nearly three hours long. Leonardo DiCaprio attended the premiere and by the end his date was too old for him. Even Prince Andrew was like, "Come on, Leo, mate. You're nearly fifty-something."

It's the last time, who cares? Apple roared into the TV game with *The Morning Show*, a superb drama about the importance of dignity and doing the right thing, made by a company that runs sweatshops in China. Well, you say you're woke but the companies you work for in China—unbelievable. Apple, Amazon, Disney. If ISIS started a streaming service you'd call your agent, wouldn't you?

So if you do win an award tonight, don't use it as a platform to make a political speech. You're in no position to lecture the public about anything. You know nothing about the real world. Most of you spent less time in school than Greta Thunberg.

So if you win, come up, accept your little award, thank your agent, and your God and f**k off, OK? It's already three hours long. Right, let's do the first award.

Overcoming a Caustic Attitude

People who have a caustic attitude toward others are often unlikely to change. The main reason is that they don't see themselves as being caustic. They see themselves as "telling it like it is," being a "straight shooter," and unwilling to be "politically correct." Seeing themselves that way keeps them in denial that they are nothing more than a mean-spirited human being who has taken being caustic to a whole new level. Nevertheless, if a person is interested in overcoming a caustic attitude, here are some tips on how they could go about it.

Ask People to Let You Know When You are Being Caustic. No one with a caustic attitude should be the one deciding if they're caustic. They are the least likely person to be honest with themselves about it. If you want to overcome being caustic, give people you trust permission to tell you when they find your words to be mean and hurtful.

Ask People to Tell You How Your Words Hurt Them. Not only do caustic people need to give others permission to say when words are caustic, they need to give people permission to express how it feels to be talked to that way. Caustic people are often out of touch with having empathy for how their words wound those they were spoken to. If you are prone to speak harshly to others, give them permission to let you know when it happens and how they felt about it. Then, and only then, might the relationship be healed.

Try to Shift to Kinder Words. Sometimes, we don't stop to realize just how harsh our words can be. Because we think we are simply telling it like it is, we think our words are fine because they honestly express how we feel. Honestly expressing how you feel doesn't mean you aren't being abusive. Think about shifting over to words that are accurate but gentler and kinder.

Think About Where Your Hurtful Words are Coming From. We have an expression in counseling: "hurt people hurt people." If you're caustic in your words and actions toward others, you have probably been treated in a similar manner along the way. Obviously, two wrongs don't make a right, so it isn't okay to hurt people with your words because others have been hurtful to you. Take a minute to think about who has been verbally abusive to you and may have role-modeled that it is okay to be that way toward others.

If you need to, get into counseling to work through who you're really angry at so you don't wound those around you.

Put Your Caustic Words in the Form of a Request. Try to take all the hostility you feel toward someone, figure out what you need from them that you're not getting, and make a *request* as to what you need. Instead of saying, "You're the most selfish and conceited person on the planet," say "I would like more of your time and attention." As the old saying goes, you catch more flies with honey than you do with vinegar.

I hope these tips are helpful. If you struggle with a caustic attitude, I hope you will act on these tips so that you become more like honey than vinegar.

Some Final Words

While it could have turned out much worse, I'm glad I had the experience I did trying to acid-wash my garage floor. Ever since it happened, it has been a painful reminder of just how corrosive words can be to the human soul. Yes, even though the muriatic acid could have damaged my lungs, I'm glad I had an up-close and personal experience with such a corrosive substance. It got my attention on a physical level and has motivated me to avoid being corrosive on a relational level.

When we treat people in a caustic manner, we are corroding their souls. We all need to get better at saying words that uplift and encourage others, not tear them down and discourage them.

Think About It

1. What people do you have a caustic, mean-spirited attitude toward?

2. What words do you use when you are being caustic?

3. What kinder and gentler words could you substitute for your caustic words that would still get your point across?

Chapter 13

People Are No Darn Good:
A Cynical Attitude

> On Monday mornings I am dedicated to the proposition
> that all men are created jerks.
>
> —H. Allen Smith

> Above all, you must understand that in the last days scoffers
> will come, scoffing and following their own evil desires.
>
> —2 Peter 3:3

Humanistic psychology teaches that people are basically good—loving, kind, giving, selfless, and . . . well, awesome. This view believes that when you try to help people struggling with psychological problems you simply offer them unconditional positive regard and unfettered acceptance and all their inborn wonderfulness will flow right out of them and they will make healthy and loving life choices.

The opposite view, taught by religious groups that are legalistic and shaming, is that people are basically evil and there is nothing good about them at all. This comes out of what used to be called in the old days "worm theology," where you're taught to think of yourself as a totally wretched human being and needed to walk around covered in sackcloth and ashes.

From my perspective, both views have it wrong.

I believe people's natural *bent* as far as their behavior is bad, meaning that we come into the world with a fallen *predisposition* to engage in what are called the "seven deadly sins": vainglory (pridefully believing you are superior to others), greed (the desire to possess more than you need), lust (inordinate or illicit sexual desire), envy (covetous of the traits, abilities, and possessions of others), gluttony (overconsumption, primarily related to food and alcohol), wrath (uncontrolled feelings of anger and rage), and sloth (being lazy and unwilling to exert sufficient effort to get things done or grow as a human being). Each of these seven destructive inclinations can be overcome by working diligently on the seven corresponding virtues of humility, charity, chastity, gratitude, temperance, patience, and diligence.

At the same time, because we are made by God in his image (*imago Dei*), we come into the world with many wonderful qualities and have inherent worth and value. Given that we are made in God's image, we have a mind (our "thinker"), emotions (our "feeler"), a will (our "chooser"), our senses (taste, touch, smell, sight, and sound), creativity (the ability to create new and unique ideas), meant for relationships (wired for deep and long-lasting intimate relationships), and spiritual beings (our immaterial, transcendent self that will never perish). If you're walking around thinking and feeling that there is nothing about you that is wonderful and worthwhile, you're dead wrong.

More than a few of us bounce back and forth between humanistic psychology and worm theology when it comes to how we view ourselves and others. Sometimes, we think we're the most awesome thing since sliced bread and that there is absolutely nothing wrong with us. At other times, we think we are a waste of human flesh, have nothing of worth or value to offer the world, and that we should jump off the nearest bridge. Both views are a gross distortion when it comes to how to view yourself and will keep you from living life well.

In this chapter, I want to focus on the latter view—that there is nothing about you or anyone else that is good or worthwhile. This overly negative view of people leads to one of the worst attitudes we can have, a cynical attitude where we see people as no darn good and that leads you to treat people rudely and dismissively.

Let me take you into the life of someone who didn't see himself or others as being made in the image of God and was overly down on himself and everyone else. The view he had of people made him hard to be around, a deeply cynical human being who didn't treat himself or anyone else with respect and dignity.

The Cynic

Diogenes of Sinope ring a bell? I didn't think so.

Diogenes was a Greek philosopher who was one of the founders of Cynic philosophy. His biography is pretty sketchy, and we don't know how much of what is said about him is true. He is believed to have been forced to leave his hometown of Sinope because either he or his father defaced the local currency. He moved to Athens where he famously lived in a wine tub for a home. Diogenes took Socratic wisdom to an extreme and lived what we would call a "low rent" life, begging for money, sleeping and eating wherever he wished, and frequently violating accepted social and religious norms.

Diogenes apparently antagonized the heck out of one of the greatest philosophers to ever walk the planet, Plato. He regularly criticized Plato, disputed Plato's interpretation of Socrates, and disrupted his lectures by bringing food to them and eating loudly, leading Plato to describe Diogenes as "a Socrates gone mad." Diogenes was an utterly shameless man who believed that if an act were not wrong *in private*, that same act is not wrong *in public*. Consequently, he did a lot of indecent things in public. Given that I want to keep this book PG, I will leave it up to you to figure out what they were.

Diogenes is said to have even insulted Alexander the Great. Alexander came to meet him one day and inquired if there was anything he could do for Diogenes. Diogenes, being an outdoorsy kind of guy who liked to use nature to toughen up his skin, replied, "Yes, stand out of my sunlight." He had no tolerance for social conventions, lived a life of poverty, acted in inappropriate ways in public, didn't care what others thought of him, and considered people's social niceties to be them hiding their dark and evil side.

Diogenes most well-known act of cynicism was walking the streets of Athens in the light of day carrying a lantern looking for one honest man. You get the implication, right? Given that a lantern in the light of day can't illuminate anything, Diogenes was letting everyone in Athens know that there wasn't an honest person among them. If you were looking for a friend back in the time of Diogenes, he wouldn't have been a good choice. With friends like him, who needed any enemies?

People of his day found Diogenes so offensive that he was called a "downright dog." This label so pleased him that he had the figure of a dog carved on the headstone for his tomb. He believed that the path to true freedom and happiness required complete honesty and total austerity. And, honest he was. When Lysias the pharmacist asked him if he believed in gods, Diogenes replied, "How can I help believing in them when I see a god-forsaken wretch life you?" When asked about the right time to marry, Diogenes replied, "For a young man not yet, for an old man never at all. Diogenes had a great fondness for freedom of speech but probably needed to work on his people skills.

Back in the time of Diogenes, cynic philosophy was a reaction to hypocrisy and corruption in politics and excesses in how people lived their lives. In today's world, it has been weaponized in that it only sees the negative in people and assumes that even people's nicest actions are motivated by selfishness. In other words, people are no darn good and never do anything for altruistic reasons. Journalist H. L. Mencken said, "A cynic is a man who smells flowers and looks around for a coffin." Social reformer Henry Ward Beecher observed, "The cynic is one who never sees a good quality in a man, and never fails to see a bad one. He is the human owl, vigilant in darkness and blind to light, mousing for vermin, and never seeing noble game." That about captures it.

Where does our cynical attitude come from? It probably comes from a number of places, but I think comedian George Carlin figured out a big piece of it when he observed, "Inside every cynical person, there is a disappointed idealist." I agree. I think our cynicism often comes from being idealistic about how human beings *should* be, running into the reality of just how fallen we truly are, and going over to the dark side of thinking that no one has anything good about them at all and never does anything out of loving and caring motives. Stephen Colbert was correct to observe, "Cynicism masquerades as wisdom, but it is the furthest thing from it. Because cynics don't learn anything. Because cynicism is self-imposed blindness: a rejection of the world because we are afraid it will hurt or disappoint us."

We pay a huge price for being cynical. Our lives shrink rather than expand, and we isolate rather than engage. Documentary filmmaker Ken Burns put it this way, "I think we too often make choices based on the safety of cynicism, and what we're led to is a life not fully lived. Cynicism is fear, and it's worse than fear—it's an active disengagement."

The cynic is usually on the outside looking in, choosing not to fully participate in life. This leads us away from engaging with others and trying to leave the world better off. Author Stephen Covey rightly challenged all of us cynics to "Be a light, not a judge, be a model not a critic. Little by little, your circle of influence will explode and you will avoid the emotional metastasizing cancers of complaining, criticizing, competing, comparing and cynicism, all which reflect victimization, all of which are the opposite of being proactive."

I find myself being cynical at times about all kinds of people and organizations—politicians, world leaders, pastors, authors, public speakers, institutions of higher education, seminaries, religious folks, counselors . . . you name it. When I'm in cynical attitude mode, I see nothing but negative qualities and dark motives. Along with my cynicism is the even more cynical belief that none of these people or groups will ever change for the better. That is why I took (painfully) to Robert Reich's words, "Cynicism is the last refuge of those who don't want to do the work of creating a better society." It is all too easy to be critical of the defects in others and in society and use one's cynicism as a hall pass to not have to roll up your sleeves and make the world a better place.

Maybe we can agree that a cynical attitude is a bad thing and something we need to work hard to overcome. My experience is that a cynical attitude is one of the toughest to overcome because we often go out each day looking for evidence in people's actions to support it. Nevertheless, let's talk about how to move away from a cynical attitude toward one that doesn't run from what is flawed and negative about people but doesn't camp out there.

Overcoming a Cynical Attitude

Like all the other bad attitudes, a cynical attitude is a tough thing to overcome. Far too often, we train our minds to think in a certain way such that it becomes deeply embedded in the way we view reality. Still, it ain't over "'til the fat lady sings" when it comes to changing our attitude. Here are some tips for how to grow out of a cynical attitude.

Acknowledge Your Inner Cynic. As with all the other bad attitudes, we are often in denial that we think the way we do. As they say, "Denial isn't a river in Egypt." We need to stop denying that we are cynical about certain things in life and courageously admit we are.

Identify What You Are Cynical About. Few of us are cynical across the board. We might be relatively free of cynicism about certain things while semi-completely cynical about others things. Take a minute to figure out the three things in life that you are the most cynical about. It helps to know what the specific objects of your cynicism are so you can zero in on those areas to form a more balanced view.

Look for the Good. I know we have gone here before, but part of overcoming any bad attitude is going to come down to accentuating the positive about people, organizations, companies, and the government. Whenever you find yourself being cynical, take a minute to think about the good things that person or organization possesses. Write the good things down and pay as much attention to them as you do the bad.

Watch and Read More Balanced News Sources. Something that feeds my cynicism is watching or reading too much from news sources that play into my cynicism. I've had to challenge myself to switch from television and print media that are unbalanced and dishonest to those that have a more balanced, truth-seeking agenda. If you want to challenge yourself to overcome your cynicism even faster, watch or read things that argue the *opposite* of how you view reality. The bottom line here is to make sure you avoid watching or reading things that only serve to strengthen your "confirmation bias" that people are no darn good. Dedicate yourself to listening to people and organizations who believe in telling the truth, the whole truth, and nothing but the truth, so help them God.

Avoid Being Around Other Cynical People. As I've said before, bad company corrupts good morals. The company you keep makes a big difference in whether or not you will be able to overcome any of the bad attitudes we explore in this book. If you have a bent toward being cynical, try to avoid being around cynical people who only reinforce your cynical attitude.

A cynical attitude is no way to go through life. While I don't want any of us to have an *overly* naïve and optimistic attitude about things, we sure can't afford to go through life dripping with cynicism. I hope the tips we just explored will be helpful to you.

Some Final Thoughts

A cynical attitude is a choice. That's why journalist John Callaway was right to challenge us to "Refuse to be cynical. Refuse to think that things can never change."

As a person who can be pretty cynical, I want to challenge all of us to work harder to overcome cynicism in life. Let's refuse to believe that people are no darn good, never do anything out of altruistic motives, can't change for the better, and doing nothing to leave the world better off. Let's start believing people have inherent worth as image bearers, perform acts of kindness for altruistic reasons, are capable of changing in a healthy direction, and doing things to leave the world better off.

Think About It

1. Who or what are you the most cynical about in terms of focusing only on the negative and assuming the worst?

2. What things about yourself are you cynical about and believe will never change?

3. What, if anything, are you doing to actively bring about positive change in yourself, others, or the world at large? Where are you being a light not a judge, a model not a critic, in your interaction with others?

The Transformative Twelve

Chapter 14

On the Sunny Side of the Street:
A Cheerful Attitude

The sovereign voluntary path to cheerfulness, if our spontaneous cheerfulness be lost, is to sit up cheerfully, to look round cheerfully, and to act and speak as if cheerfulness were already there.

—William James

The days of the oppressed are wretched, but
the cheerful heart has a continual feast.

—Proverbs 15:15

I hate to admit it, but I find cheerful people irritating. I say that knowing that there is something wrong with *me* that I feel this way. Something about having spent my life being melancholic plays a big part here, but truth be told, when I am around *overly* cheerful people, the hair stands up on the back of my neck and I can't get away fast enough.

Nevertheless, a cheerful attitude is crucial in living life well. You never want to leave home without one. This reminds me of an iconic song, *On the Sunny Side of the Street*, that encouraged people to make sure they attitudinally walk on the side of the street that is sunny and bright with the good things in life, rather than than the dark and gloomy side of the street, focusing on the bad. By the way, that song was written in 1930s in the midst of the Great Depression, one of the worst times in our country's history.

THE TRANSFORMATIVE TWELVE

Let me take you into the life of one of the most cheerful people I know, someone whose friendship I greatly value. His friendship has been a godsend and great blessing to my life. Without it, I can't imagine how melancholic and cheerless I would be.

Tigger and Eeyore

Amir, my close friend for over twenty-five years now, is a naturally cheerful guy. I believe he came into the world with a smile on his face. Amir is what I call a "trait cheerful" person. It's just how he's wired. One of his favorite books (other than my books, of course, which I make him read whether he wants to or not) is *Herbie's Happy Day*, a children's book. That's Amir—always happy, cheerful, and upbeat.

I, on the other hand, did not come into the world with the cheerful trait. I came into the world with the uncheerful trait. If there were such a book, my favorite would be *Herbie's Unhappy, Cheerless Day*. I wouldn't know what it is like to be cheerful if it came up and bit me on the nose. Why Amir has anything to do with me is beyond me. I think he sees me as a reclamation project.

If Amir and I were cast in a *Winnie the Pooh* movie, Amir would be Tigger and I would be Eeyore. If you have ever read *Winnie the Pooh* or watched the cartoons or movies, you know that Tigger is a cheerful, friendly, outgoing, overly confident and optimistic tiger who is especially known for his love of bouncing. Always referring to himself in the third person, Tigger says things like "Tiggers don't jump, they bounce!" "Bouncy trouncy flouncy pouncy fun fun fun fun fun," and "Well, I gotta go now! I got a lot of bouncing to do! Hoo-hoo-hoo-hoo!"

Eeyore, on the other hand, is this constantly gloomy, pessimistic, sky-is-falling donkey who doesn't bounce around from place to place but sulks and pouts from place to place. The interesting thing in Winnie the Pooh stories is that in spite of how different Tigger and Eeyore are, they become best friends. I think they need each other to balance their personalities. Tigger needs Eeyore to help him be a little less *overly* cheerful, bouncy, and confident, and Eeyore needs Tigger to help him be a little less overly gloomy, sad, and pessimistic. They are a match made in heaven, but I'm sure Tigger and Eeyore drive each other nuts at times.

Amir and I need each other for the very same reasons. Let me drive this home by taking you out onto the golf course.

Amir and I love golf. Absolutely love it. We have played hundreds of rounds of golf together. But we have much different playing styles. Amir steps out onto a golf course brimming with confidence, sure he is going to shoot a great score every time. I, on the other hand, step out on a golf course hoping no one is watching, sure that I'm going to top the ball on the first tee and watch it dribble a few yards in front of me, and feeling that I will be lucky if I don't injure myself during the round, given how horrible my swing is.

Amir is constantly encouraging me that I can pull off a particularly difficult shot and often tells me to try the riskier shot rather than play it safe. If I had a nickel for every time he told me "You can do it," I would be a rich man. I, on the other hand, am always trying to talk Amir down from trying to hit shots that only Tiger Woods can hit. God love him, Amir thinks he can make shots even the professionals know they would be lucky to hit.

I'm never going to be a Tigger and Amir is never going to be an Eeyore. But, I'm very thankful to him for showing me what a genuinely cheerful person looks like and certainly want to move more in that direction each day. I hope he feels the same way about me in that he wants to tap the brakes a little when it comes to being *overly* optimistic and confident about the kinds of things he can do on a golf course.

If you come by a cheerful attitude naturally, I'm happy for you (not really; again, I find you irritating). If you are like me and are rarely cheerful, I want to encourage you to keep working on developing a more cheerful attitude during the limited amount of time you have on this miserable planet (okay, it's not a miserable planet).

If you resist working on a more cheerful attitude, you are only emotionally harming yourself and negatively affecting those around you. I know the healthy, loving side of you doesn't want to do that. The healthy part of you doesn't want to rain on your own parade while you're here, nor rain on the parade of others. On that encouraging note, here are my thoughts about how to develop a cheerful attitude.

Developing a Cheerful Attitude

There are probably a million ways to develop a cheerful attitude. Here are some possibilities for you to think about.

Commit to Being Cheerful. Martha Washington, the wife of our first president, said "I am determined to be cheerful and happy in whatever situation I may find myself. For I have learned that the greater part of our misery or unhappiness is determined not by our circumstance but by our disposition." As rough as she and George had it while trying to pull off the greatest start-up country of all time, Martha willed herself to be cheerful about life no matter what bad things came her way. That's the attitude we all need to have more of, don't you think?

Understand What Being Cheerful Is and Is Not About. Developing a cheerful attitude *is not* about being out of touch with the painful and darker realities of life or trying to talk yourself into seeing everything as wonderful and awesome. As newspaper columnist Mike Royko put it, "Show me somebody who is always smiling, always cheerful, always optimistic, and I will show you somebody who hasn't the faintest idea what the heck is really going on." A cheerful attitude is not a "I'm walking on sunshine" attitude. It is a commitment to focus the vast majority of your attention on the things in life that are *truly* positive, upbeat, and good. If you have a cheerful attitude, you're not *walking* on sunshine; you're walking *in* sunshine.

Engage Your Body, Especially Your Face. I've been told that I have a serious, non-cheerful face. I don't appreciate people telling me that, but that's what I've been told. If we are going to become cheerful people in attitude, we have to be cheerful in body. Mother Teresa had it right when she said, "Speak tenderly; let there be kindness in your face, in your eyes, in your smile, in the warmth of your greeting. Always have a cheerful smile." Go back to the William James quote at the top of the chapter, where he wisely encourages us "to sit up cheerfully, to look round cheerfully, and to act and speak as if cheerfulness were already there." This reminds me of another song, "When You're Smiling (The Whole World Smiles with You)." Guess when it was written—1928, at the start of the Great Depression.

Work on a Cheerful Attitude by Trying to Help Others Be Cheerful. Mark Twain said, "The best way to cheer yourself up is to try to cheer somebody else up." Get out of yourself and your own internal dreariness and try to brighten someone else's day. English banker and politician John Lubbock noted, "Everyone must have felt a cheerful friend is like a sunny day, which sheds its brightness on all around." As I mentioned earlier, Amir is my cheerful best friend. If Charles Kingsley is right, that "The men whom I have seen succeed best in life always have been cheerful and hopeful men; who went about their business with a smile on their faces; and took the changes and chances of this mortal life like men; facing rough and smooth alike as it came," Amir is succeeding best in life. Personally, I want to return the favor to him and all my family and friends by trying to cheer them up whenever I can.

Keep Cheerfulness and Circumstances Separate from Each Other.

Writer and theologian G. K. Chesterton wisely notes, "Hope is the power of being cheerful in circumstances *which we know to be desperate*" [italics mine]. Roberto Benigni's powerful movie *Life is Beautiful* comes to mind. It is about a father maintaining a cheerful attitude in front of his son as the two of them try to survive the desperate circumstance of being in a Nazi concentration camp. The father turns being in a truly evil and dark situation into a game to shield his son from the horrors of what is happening around them, no small task to say the least.

Some people see their job as a watered-down form of a concentration camp but would be wise to take a cheerful attitude with them to work each day. Writer Stephen Lundin rightly notes, "When we come to [work] we bring an attitude. We can bring a moody attitude and have a depressing day. We can bring a grouchy attitude and irritate our coworkers and customers. Or we can bring a sunny, playful, cheerful attitude and have a great day."

A cheerful attitude is to be kept completely separate from the circumstances we experience day to day. As writer Max Ehrmann notes, "With all its sham, drudgery, and broken dreams, it is still a beautiful world. Be cheerful."

As I said earlier, there are numerous ways to develop a cheerful attitude other than the five we just covered. I hope these were helpful.

Some Final Thoughts

I highly recommend that we work on developing a cheerful attitude as we go through life, especially those of us who don't come by it naturally. Study after study and article after article make a compelling case for how important a cheerful spirit is for us.

Cheerfulness is good for us medically in that it reduces the risk of heart disease and other ailments. Proverbs 17:22 agrees, saying, "A cheerful heart is good medicine, but a crushed spirit dries up the bones."

A cheerful attitude is good for us relationally. Cheerful people make friends better and maintain those friendships longer. There is a lot of truth to poet Ella Wheeler Wilcox's statement, "Laugh and the world laughs with you; cry and you cry alone."

Finally, a cheerful attitude is good for us spiritually. It keeps us from falling into being resentful, bitter, and unappreciative when God allows (not causes) life to throw us some pretty painful circumstances.

Whether you're a Tigger, an Eeyore, or somewhere in between, let's all commit to developing a cheerful attitude, one based in the reality that while things are hard and painful to some degree here on earth, we have so much to be thankful for and optimistic about as we live our lives. The glass of life really isn't half full or half empty, it is overflowing given all the good and wonderful things we are blessed with, something that ought to put a huge smile on our face and lead us to spread good cheer to others.

Think About It

1. What part of your life do you have the hardest time being cheerful about?

2. Is there a person in your life who brings out the cheerful side of you? Describe him or her.

3. Who is someone you could cheer up and how would you do it?

Chapter 15

Go All In: A Committed Attitude

> Commitment is what transforms a promise into a reality . . . Commitment is the stuff character is made of; the power to change the face of things. It is the daily triumph of integrity over skepticism.
>
> —Abraham Lincoln

> Commit to the Lord whatever you do, and he will establish your plans.
>
> —Proverbs 16:3

I'm sure you have heard the humorous statement, "The difference between involvement and commitment is like the difference between eggs and bacon. The chicken is involved and the pig is committed." Corny, I know, but true.

Without commitment, none of us are going to amount to much. Unless you go all in, you won't be able to leave yourself or the world around you a whole lot better off. You have to decide if you are going to be a chicken or a pig as you go through life and what you are going sacrificially devote your life to accomplishing. Rick Warren was right when he said, "Nothing shapes your life more than the commitments you choose to make."

In light of the importance of commitment, I want to take you into the lives of three women who made a commitment, who went all in, and left the world a much better place. We would be wise to follow their examples.

The Hidden Women of NASA

I watched the movie *Hidden Figures* recently and was deeply moved by it. In case you don't know, the movie is about three women, Katherine Johnson, Dorothy Vaughn, and Mary Jackson, who worked for NASA (known as NACA, the National Advisory Committee for Aeronautics, at the time) in the 1950s and 1960s. The movie focuses on the challenges the women faced being African-American and female during a time when racism and sexism were alive and well.

Because there was a shortage of men during World War II, NASA hired women with college degrees in mathematics to work as "human computers" and help with the all the number crunching that needed to be done. Even though they did the same work as their white counterparts, African-American women were paid less, housed in a separate location on the NASA campus, and had to use a bathroom and dining facility for "colored" people.

Dorothy Vaughn was one of NASA's first "human computers" and became its first black supervisor and an expert in computer programming. Mary Jackson graduated from college with dual degrees in math and physical science. She became NASA's first African-American female engineer.

The key figure in the movie is Katherine Johnson. She graduated from high school at the age of fourteen and college at the age of eighteen in mathematics and French. She joined NASA in 1953 and worked there for thirty-five years. Her job included calculating launch windows, emergency return paths, and trajectories for the Mercury and Apollo spaceflights.

President Obama awarded Johnson the Presidential Medal of Freedom in 2015, one of the highest honors our country can bestow on a civilian. In 2016, a new research building on the NASA campus was named the Katherine G. Johnson Computational Research Facility in her honor.

What I find amazing about these three women was their level of commitment to their job. Everyone at NASA worked long and grueling hours to accomplish their mission of putting a man in space (women weren't allowed to go into space yet). This had to be especially difficult for women who were black. They were underpaid, overworked, not allowed to use the "white" bathrooms, ignored by colleagues, dismissively talked down to, and not allowed to put their names on reports. In the face of that, their level of commitment was severely tested each and every day.

John Wesley said, "Do all the good you can, by all the means you can, in all the ways you can, in all the places you can, at all the times you can, to all the people you can, as long as ever you can." That's what Kathryn, Dorothy, and Mary did. They went all in, devoted themselves to doing their jobs at the highest level of excellence possible, and left an indelible mark on NASA. They endured racism and sexism, took the higher ground, and left the world a better place.

As we saw at the top of this chapter, Abraham Lincoln said, "Commitment is what transforms a promise into a reality . . . Commitment is the stuff character is made of; the power to change the face of things. It is the daily triumph of integrity over skepticism." I wonder if Lincoln could have ever imagined in his wildest dreams that there would come a day a hundred years after he kept the country from tearing itself apart over slavery that three African American women would be leading us into space.

Developing a Committed Attitude

I want to use the movie *Hidden Figures* to give you some tips on how to develop an attitude of commitment. Kathryn Johnson, Dorothy Vaughn, and Mary Jackson did each of the things listed below, and it strengthened their commitment to their work at NASA.

Work Together and Support Each Other. To be committed to a cause, you have to work collaboratively with others. You can't be a Lone Ranger who is keeping others at arm's length and riding solo. Throughout the movie, Kathryn, Dorothy, and Mary were there for each other, encouraging each other's personal and professional growth. They could not have done it without each other's consistent emotional support.

Work Through Conflicts. In the movie, Kathryn, Dorothy, and Mary ran into conflicts with people at NASA and in their local community because of the racism and sexism that was rampant. Many of the people at the space agency at the time were outright hostile to these women. Each woman did what she could to work through the conflict they had with the powers that be, and came out on the other side being a role model for what commitment looks like.

Have Fun and Play Together. Kathryn, Dorothy, and Mary knew how to have fun and celebrate with each other and their loved ones. No one they worked for at NASA at the time was going to have fun with them, so they turned to each other and their families for times of enjoyment and laughter so they could live to fight another day.

Overcome Obstacles and Learn from Mistakes. Each woman ran into obstacles when working at NASA, whether it was related to how they were being treated or just the obstacles they encountered in facing the specific tasks they were given to do. Rather than allow obstacles to discourage them or a setback to defeat them, they each overcame barriers in front of them and grew from the setbacks they faced.

Challenge Yourself to Take the Next Step. Commitment means not "settling" for where you are or what you have accomplished. Kathryn, Dorothy, and Mary saw what was ahead of them and did the necessary study, training, and work to move forward. None of them rested on their laurels. Instead, they kept focusing on how they could grow as professionals and as human beings. In my line of work, we say that you are either moving forward or moving backward. These three amazing women were always moving forward.

There are many more ways to work on developing a committed attitude. I hope these five tips help motivate you to keep strengthening your commitment to worthwhile endeavors in life. In all this, I'm reminded of Winston Churchill's famous statement, "Never give in. Never give in. Never, never, never, never—in nothing, great or small, large or petty—never give in, except to convictions of honour and good sense. Never yield to force. Never yield to the apparently overwhelming might of the enemy." Katherine Johnson, Dorothy Vaughn, and Mary Jackson showed all of us, regardless of skin color or gender, what commitment looks like, the kind that leads you to never give up and never give in.

Some Final Thoughts

Each day our level of commitment in life is going to be challenged. Motivational speaker Zig Ziglar noted, "It was character that got us out of bed, commitment that moved us into action, and discipline that enabled us to follow through." Think about that. Character got you out of bed this morning, the part of you that believes in living your life according to your core values. Commitment moved you into action, the part of you that understands "commitment is an act, not a word" (Jean-Paul Sartre). And discipline, the part of you that chooses to persevere in doing the right thing, enabled you to follow through.

One of Dr. Martin Luther King, Jr.'s most oft-quoted statements was "I have a dream that my four little children will one day live in a nation where they will not be judged by the color of their skin, but by the content of their character." Because of the high level of their character, commitment, and discipline, NASA ultimately judged Katherine Johnson, Dorothy Vaughn, and Mary Jackson by the content of their character and not the color of their skin. Their unflinching commitment to their work under extremely difficult circumstances made all the difference in the world, for them and for us.

Think About It

1. Looking back on your life, where did you give your full commitment? How did things turn out?

2. What goal or vision have you had for your life where your commitment level was lacking? How did that turn out?

3. Looking to the future, what area of your life do you need to go "all in" so that you can achieve something meaningful and leave the world better off?

Chapter 16

Walk in Their Shoes:
A Compassionate Attitude

> Compassion asks us to go where it hurts, to enter into the places of
> pain, to share in brokenness, fear, confusion, and anguish. Compassion
> challenges us to cry out with those in misery, to mourn with those
> who are lonely, to weep with those in tears. Compassion requires us to
> be weak with the weak, vulnerable with the vulnerable, and powerless
> with the powerless. Compassion means full immersion in the condi-
> tion of being human.

—Henri Nouwen

> Therefore, as God's chosen people, holy and dearly loved, clothe your-
> selves with compassion, kindness, humility, gentleness and patience.

—Colossians 3:12

Compassion seems to be in short supply these days. Sometimes, it takes an incendiary event to get people stirred up enough to march on the streets and act on the compassion they feel about people being mistreated.

The murder of George Floyd, a black man, at the hands of a white po-lice officer, was such an event. Floyd's murder set off a firestorm of protest in our country and had people marching in the streets in a way we haven't seen since the Vietnam War protests of the late 1960s and early 1970s. It has been encouraging to see a wide variety of Americans protesting against the mistreatment that people of color have experienced in our country. The compassion many have expressed gives me hope that we will continue to overcome the ills of the past.

Let me take you into the life of a person who epitomized compassion for the pain others experienced. She stands as a testimony to how much good someone can do when they have true empathy for the suffering of others.

The Abolitionist

She was born in Litchfield, Connecticut on June 14, 1811, the seventh of thirteen children. Her father was a preacher, and her mother a deeply religious woman who passed away when she was five. At the age of twenty-one, she moved to Cincinnati to join her father, who had become the president of Lane Theological Seminary. There, she met the man who would become her husband, who was a professor at the seminary. They had seven children together. Her husband was an ardent critic of slavery, and the two of them supported the Underground Railroad, a network of secret routes and safe houses used by slaves in the south to escape into the free states of the north.

She claimed to have had a vision of a dying slave during communion at a church service that prompted her to write about the plight of slaves in the United States. What also may have prompted her to write about slavery was the death of her eighteen-month-old son, about whom she said, "Having experienced losing someone so close to me, I can sympathize with all the poor, powerless slaves at the unjust auctions." She was referring, of course, to the inhuman practice of auctioning off slaves that led to husbands and wives being separated from each other, parents being separated from their children, and children being separated from their siblings.

Her book on the plight of slaves was published in installments in the newspaper *The National Era*. The original subtitle was *The Man That Was a Thing*. The purpose of her writings was to educate northerners of the horrors of what was happening in the South and to make people in the South more compassionate toward those they forced into slavery. To say her writings touched off of firestorm of controversy and vitriol would be a gross understatement. The serialization of her writings was published in full book form in 1852.

Her book sold an unprecedented 300,000 copies at the time, was the largest selling novel of the nineteenth century, and was the second-bestselling book of the century after the Bible. Her compassion about slavery compelled her to help people better understand how slavery not only negatively impacted the masters, traders, and slaves but everyone in society. She deeply understood what Thomas Merton would later write: "The whole idea of compassion is based on a keen awareness of the interdependence of all these living beings, which are all part of one another, and all involved in one another." Her novel led to a meeting with President Abraham Lincoln on November 25, 1862, during which her son said that Lincoln greeted her by saying, "So you're the little woman who wrote the book that started this great war."

All this because one person had compassion toward the desperate plight of others. Harriet Beecher Stowe, whose novel *Uncle Tom's Cabin* helped change a country, had compassion toward those subjected to slavery in the South, and the country began to move in a different and better direction.

Compassion is the ability to approach other people's problems as if they are your own, have empathy and sympathy for how others suffer, have other people's backs even though you're not going through what they are, face violent opposition rather than run from it, find something in common with others even if your suffering isn't as bad, understand that people have differences of opinion but to stand up for what is right, believe that knowledge about someone else's plight is wasted if you don't share it, and not give up even though others will try to defeat everything you're doing.

The *real* movers and shakers in human history have always been the people who had compassion for the suffering of others around them. Harriet Beecher Stowe had that. Her interactions with slaves fleeing the South and the loss of her child helped her get there, but those experiences had to encounter a soft heart that hadn't become hardened by indifference or callousness about the suffering of others. Harriet Beecher Stowe had a tender and soft heart when it came to the suffering of slaves in our country and the right experiences to turn her into one of the most influential figures in American history.

You can't be a mover and a shaker sitting on your duff. Even if your contribution is relatively small compared to others, you have to take action by channeling your compassion into doing something that helps correct the wrong that disturbs your soul.

Developing an Attitude of Compassion

You don't need me to tell you that the world needs more people who have compassion for the oppressed and downtrodden. We've already explored how a callous attitude toward people is destroying the world we live in. Here are some tips on how to cultivate an attitude of compassion so we can heal our world and bring it back to life.

Walk in Their Shoes. We are going to come back to this tip time and time again. We need to take time each day to stop and have empathy for what others are going through, whether it is losing a job, the death of a loved one, or struggling with a serious addiction. We need to get out of ourselves long enough to feel the pain of others and have compassion for their struggles.

Grieve with Those Who Grieve. All of us suffer painful losses in life. When those losses come, we need people to come alongside and grieve with us. We have to mourn with those who mourn and have compassion for how gut-wrenching some loses are in life. Shed tears with those who shed tears. Put your arm around them. Let them know that they will be able to get on the other side of their loss or setback sooner or later. Weep with those who weep.

Bear Their Burden. Everyone is responsible for facing their own problems and doing what they can to resolve them. Nevertheless, we are to bear burdens with people by offering whatever help or assistance we can. Bringing meals over, babysitting children, taking people to doctor's appointments, cleaning their house . . . there are a hundred ways we can bear someone's burdens when they are going through a rough time.

Forgive Those Who Have Hurt You. We are going to come back to this tip time and time again as well. Forgiving others requires that we feel compassion for how troubled and messed up all of us are in the way we live our lives. Forgiveness is not saying that what the person did was okay or that it didn't hurt, it's making a choice to wipe the slate clean regarding them having hurt you. Forgiveness doesn't always mean reconciling with the person who hurt you. If the person who hurt you is truly sorry and willing to make amends, reconciliation is possible. If they aren't sorry or repentant, reconciliation isn't possible and you need to keep them at arm's length. Forgive others out of compassion for how sinful and dysfunctional all of us are. You'll be doing yourself a big favor because you won't be carrying around all the bitterness and resentment you feel and will experience greater freedom to live life more fully.

Avoid Compassion Fatigue. All of us can experience what psychologists call compassion fatigue, especially those of us in the people-helping fields. It's all too easy to start hardening your heart toward others to protect yourself from the emotional pain of interacting with people who are experiencing so much suffering. Make sure you refuel your spiritual, psychological, and physical tanks often enough so you can remain compassionate when dealing with people who are hurting. Take long walks, express your own hurts to trusted friends, have fun, eat right, and keep your spiritual life up and running. Your kindness and compassion have to be recharged each day, otherwise you won't be any good to anyone, including yourself.

As with any attitude we cover, there are so many other ways to cultivate an attitude of compassion. Please, do whatever you can to avoid a hardened heart. Proverbs 4:23 says, "Above all else, guard your heart, for everything you do flows from it." Among other things, guarding your heart means having healthy boundaries with those who hurt you, doing what you can to heal the relational wounds you've already experienced, letting people do loving and kinds things for you, and doing loving and kind things for yourself.

Some Final Thoughts

They say "love makes the world go round." I don't completely agree. I think compassion makes the world go round. A person, a country, or a world that lacks compassion is ultimately not going to be loving in terms of taking action aimed at helping things improve. All the evil tyrants of history, whatever else they had in common, lacked human compassion. You have to be able to feel the pain of others and have compassion about how painful their lives are if you want to call yourself a human being.

I want to challenge all of us to work on developing greater compassion toward both ourselves and others as we live life. Notice that I said compassion toward ourselves. Brene Brown observed, "We can't practice compassion with other people if we can't treat ourselves kindly." She's right. We can't have compassion toward others if we don't have it toward ourselves first. Start in your own backyard with compassion, then you will be able to have compassion for your neighbor.

Essayist Ralph Waldo Emerson said, "The purpose of life is not to be happy. It is to be useful, to be honorable, to be compassionate, to have it make some difference that you have lived and lived well." Harriet Beecher Stowe lived that way, and that's why she made "some difference" in how she lived her life. She understood that compassion is, as Frederick Buechner so beautifully put it, "the fatal capacity for feeling what it is like to live inside somebody else's skin. It is the knowledge that there can never really be any peace and joy for me until there is peace and joy finally for you too." Harriet Beecher Stowe understood that there could never be any peace or joy for herself or our country until we had compassion for the suffering of slaves and there was peace and joy for them as free citizens of our country.

Chinese philosopher Confucius said, "Wisdom, compassion, and courage are the three universally recognized moral qualities of men." We, as human beings, have the compacity for the moral quality of compassion, but we also have the capacity for callousness and cruelty. Norman Cousins wisely noted, "The individual is capable of both great compassion and great indifference. He has it within his means to nourish the former and outgrow the latter." Let's keep working to nourish the former and outgrow the latter.

Think About It

1. Who has been hurtful to you that you have little, if any, compassion toward?

2. Whose pain (physical, psychological, and spiritual) do you find yourself having empathy and compassion toward?

3. How compassionate are you toward yourself in the face of life being difficult and painful for you?

Chapter 17

Be Satisfied with What You Have:
A Contented Attitude

> You say, "If I had a little more, I should be very satisfied." You make a mistake. If you are not content with what you have, you would not be satisfied if it were doubled.
>
> —Charles Spurgeon

> For we brought nothing into the world, and we can take nothing out of it. But if we have food and clothing, we will be content with that.
>
> —1 Timothy 6:8

Contentment. Oh, how we long for it but rarely seem to find it. Why is it so elusive? Because we fall into the trap, time and time again, of wanting what we don't have rather than wanting what we have. Philosopher Epicurus wisely noted, "Do not spoil what you have by desiring what you have not; remember that what you now have was once among the things you only hoped for." Think about that. We are only emotionally ruining our time on earth by desiring what we don't have, something that makes it impossible to be happy and content with what we have already been blessed with.

Going even further than that, Epicurus is saying that what we already have is what we had only hoped for earlier in our lives. What a horrible lie we tell ourselves when we think that happiness and contentment come from outside of us. Og Mandino was right when he observed, "Realize that true happiness lies within you. Waste no time and effort searching for peace and contentment and joy in the world outside. Remember that there is no happiness in having or in getting, but only in giving. Reach out. Share. Smile. Hug. Happiness is a perfume you cannot pour on others without getting a few drops on yourself."

I have struggled throughout my life with what Epicurus is talking about, especially when it comes to my professional life. When I got an undergraduate degree in psychology, I convinced myself I would be content if I could get a master's degree. When I got a master's degree, I convinced myself I would be content if I got a doctorate. When I got my doctorate, I convinced myself I would be content once I got my license to practice as a psychologist. Once I got my license to practice as a psychologist, I convinced myself that I would be content if my caseload was full. When my caseload was full, I convinced myself that I would be content if I could write a self-help book. Once I wrote a self-help book, I convinced myself that I would be content if I could do seminars around the country on the book. Once I was doing seminars around the country, I convinced myself that I would be content if I could get on the Oprah Winfrey show to promote my book and become famous and wealthy. Unfortunately, Oprah never called, so I am currently discontented with my professional life.

I want to take you into the lives of three iconic figures in human history, none of whom ever seemed to find inner peace or contentment. They are an object lesson for us all.

"Just a Little Bit More"

John D. Rockefeller was one of the greatest industrialists the world has ever known. He built Standard Oil into the biggest and most profitable company in the world, something that made him the richest man in the world. Rockefeller was frequently vilified in the press for his merciless business practices, once saying, "The way to make money is to buy when blood is running in the streets." At the same time, he gave away hundreds of millions of dollars to support education, medicine, and the arts. Rockefeller believed that the best use of one's life was to make as much money as possible and do the most good with it to improve the condition of mankind. When he was asked once, "How much money is enough money?," he replied "just a little bit more."

Alexander the Great succeeded his father to the throne of Macedonia, was tutored by Aristotle until the age of sixteen (can you imagine having

Aristotle for a teacher?), was undefeated in battle, was one of the world's greatest military leaders, and is considered one of the most influential people in human history. Yet, when he had conquered the known world, he wept over the possibility "Are there no more worlds that I might conquer?" As Charles Spurgeon noted, "A man's contentment is in his mind, not in the extent of his possessions." Alexander the Great, with the world at his feet, cried for another world to conquer.

Solomon is considered to be one of the wisest people who has ever lived. He was the King of Israel from 970 to 931 BCE, succeeding his father, King David, to the throne. Listen to how he describes his life:

> I undertook great projects: I built houses for myself and planted vineyards. I made gardens and parks and planted all kinds of fruit trees in them. I made reservoirs to water groves of flourishing trees. I bought male and female slaves and had other slaves who were born in my house. I also owned more herds and flocks than anyone in Jerusalem before me. I amassed silver and gold for myself, and the treasure of kings and provinces. I acquired male and female singers, and a harem as well—the delights of a man's heart. I became greater by far than anyone in Jerusalem before me. In all this my wisdom stayed with me. I denied myself nothing my eyes desired; I refused my heart no pleasure. My heart took delight in all my labor, and this was the reward for all my toil. (Ecclesiastes 2:4–10).

Solomon had a harem of 300 concubines in addition to 700 wives. You would think if anyone would be content, it would be our man Solomon. But, listen to what he says: "Yet when I surveyed all that my hands had done and what I had toiled to achieve, everything was meaningless, a chasing after the wind; nothing was gained under the sun" (Ecclesiastes 4:11).

Step back for a minute. We have an uber-wealthy industrialist who needed "just a little bit more" money, a world-class military leader who needed a few more worlds to conquer, and one of the wisest and wealthiest people who ever lived who needed a few more great projects to do. Yikes!

Vivien Greene, once the world's foremost doll house expert, said, "It is not our circumstances that create our discontent or contentment. It is us." She's right. The problem if you're discontented with your life is not what you do or don't have, it's you. The problem with John D. Rockefeller, Alexander the Great, and Solomon wasn't their circumstances. It was them. It was an internal failure to genuinely appreciate what they had in life. The Dalai Lama was spot on when he said, "When you are discontent, you always want more, more, more. Your desire can never be satisfied. But when you practice contentment, you can say to yourself, 'Oh yes—I already have everything that I really need.'" "I want just a little bit more" has to be replaced with "I already have everything that I really need."

So, all this raises the million-dollar question, "How to I learn to be more content?"

Developing a Contented Attitude

There are numerous ways we can work on becoming more contented in life. Here are five possibilities for you to consider.

Work on Being Content with Little. Isaac Bickerstaffe stated, "But if I'm content with a little, enough is as good as a feast." Think about that—if we can be content with the basics of life at whatever level we have them, we will find that more than the basics is an overwhelming feast. Had I been *content* with receiving a high school education growing up, all that came after that (getting college degrees, writing books, and giving seminars) would have been an overwhelming feast in life. Because I wasn't, it wasn't. If you develop any mantras after reading this book, I want one of them to be "Content with little."

Keep Working on an Attitude of Gratitude. Take time each day to express gratitude for all that you already have. A song I sang growing up in church, "Count Your Blessings," is something we need now more than ever. Don't neglect this key way to be content—"count your many blessings, name them one by one." Most of us *already* have so much to be thankful for such that if even more didn't come along we are already rich.

Try to Avoid Missing the Forest for the Trees. One of the ways we rain on our own parade in life is to focus on what we don't have rather than what we do. When I was a college professor, I would focus on the small number of students who were falling asleep or looking bored during a lecture rather than the majority of students who were alert, asking questions, and happy to be in my class. Don't let focusing on the smaller number of dead trees in life keep you from seeing the whole forest.

Say No to the Trinkets of This World. Some of us have pursued money, power, and sex in an effort to be happy and content in life, at the expense of the deeper and more important things like close relationships, meaningful work, and helping out those in need. Don't waste your life going after the superficial trinkets the world has to offer, no matter how pleasurable they may be. If you go after the deeper and better things, all these other things come your way to the degree that you need them.

Stop Comparing. It's hard to be content with what you have when you're always looking right or left at what everyone else has. Try not to compare your life to anyone else's. You have no idea what advantages or disadvantages they may have had in pursuing the American Dream. Don't look around you, look inside and up for what you want that is truly valuable and worth pursuing.

Yes, I know, all this is easier said than done, right? But, that's true of all the really important challenges we face in life. In general, things that are easy to do aren't worth doing. I encourage you to keep working on an attitude of contentment so that you can win twice—first, by being content with little, and, second, by truly enjoying and appreciating all that goes beyond the essentials.

Some Final Thoughts

Alfred Nobel, the inventor of dynamite and the one after whom the Nobel Prize is named, said "Contentment is the only real wealth." John D. Rockefeller may have had tremendous monetary wealth and done a lot of good with it, but he may not have ever discovered the wealth of being content. Alexander the Great may have been undefeated on the battlefield and conquered the known world, but he may not have discovered the wealth of being content. Solomon may have had all the wisdom in the world, achieved great things, acquired great wealth, and been able to sleep with anyone one he wanted to, but it ended up being a meaningless chasing after the wind because he didn't have the wealth of personal contentment. These three men, and all the rest of us who struggle with being content with what we already have, would be wise to heed the words of Oscar Wilde: "True contentment is not having everything, but in being satisfied with everything you have."

Think About It

1. Where in life are you the most discontented?

2. In that area, what do you already have that is the "little" that ought to be enough?

3. Where in life are you genuinely content?

Chapter 18

Be Sorry About Your Mistakes:
A Contrite Attitude

True repentance includes sorrow for sin and contrition of heart.
It breaks the heart with sighs and sobs and groans.

—Thomas Brooks

Godly sorrow brings repentance that leads to salvation
and leaves no regret, but worldly sorrow brings death.

—2 Corinthians 7:10

Who apologizes anymore? Let me put that better. Who *sincerely* apologizes anymore? From my perspective, there seem to be a relatively small number of people who are truly contrite and remorseful when they wound someone by doing something selfish or mean.

All this reminds me of the television show, *Happy Days*, an idealized version of life back in the mid-1950s to mid-1960s. Specifically, I'm reminded of Fonzie, the epitome of "cool" back then. Fonzie was a "rebel without a cause" kind of guy who rode a motorcycle, was a "chick magnet," and always seemed to have everything figured out.

The only problem with Fonzie is that he couldn't admit when he was wrong or say he was sorry. Literally. He couldn't get the words out of his mouth. Take a minute to view the video on YouTube, "Fonzie: I was wrorrrrr!" to see what I mean. Also, watch the video, "Funniest baby struggles to say I'm Sorry!" It'll make you laugh out loud and give you a better feel for how hard it is for all of us, even little ones, to say we're sorry when we mess up.

This issue of lacking contrition has certainly been in the news for a while now. Harvey Weinstein, Bill Cosby, Charlie Sheen, Kevin Spacey, Jeffrey Epstein, and R. Kelly have all been publicly called out for having lived lives behind the scenes that were anything but upstanding and honorable, about which they seem to have had very little if any remorse. In this chapter, I want to examine two celebrities who got caught doing something wrong and how different their reactions were when they got caught.

The Hollywood Moms Who Wanted Their Kids to Go to Elite Colleges

A story broke some time ago about fifty or so people who were involved in a college admission cheating scam aimed at getting their unqualified children into elite colleges. It came to be called the "Varsity Blues" scandal. Parents paid millions of dollars to get people to cheat on admissions tests on behalf of their children as well as to get colleges to accept their kids as athletes even though their kids didn't play a sport. SAT and ACT test administrators were bribed so they would allow a confederate to take tests for some of these kids, as were college coaches so they would portray a potential student as a recruit in their particular sport even though the kid couldn't walk and chew gum at the same time.

Two Hollywood celebrities were part of the scandal, actresses Lori Laughlin and Felicity Huffman. Laughlin and her husband, fashion designer Mossimo Giannulli, were charged with paying $500,000 in bribes to get their two daughters into the University of Southern California as crew athletes even though neither participated in the sport. Huffman was charged with participating in a scheme to falsely inflate her daughter's college entrance exam score by paying $15,000 to arrange for a test monitor to correct wrong answers.

A lot of people were disgusted by what happened, and these celebrities were scorched in the press and on social media. The FBI arrested both of these celebrities, something that had to be embarrassing and traumatic. Huffman pled guilty to the charges, expressed remorse, and has served her time, while Loughlin and Giannulli initially pled not guilty and fought the charges in an effort to stay out of jail.

I admire what Huffman said after she pled guilty: "I am pleading guilty to the charge brought against me by the United States Attorney's Office. I am in full acceptance of my guilt, and with deep regret and shame over what I have done, I accept full responsibility for my actions and will accept the consequences that stem from those action." Loughlin and her husband, on the other hand, initially argued that they didn't know they were doing anything wrong, as if that is ever a good defense. The next time you get pulled over for speeding, tell the cop, "Officer, I didn't know I was speeding!" and see how that works out for you.

I had already finished this chapter when there was a recent development in the Varsity Blues scandal. Loughlin and Giannulli finally agreed to plead guilty to the charges. The general consensus of opinion is that they saw the handwriting on the wall that they faced much longer prison sentences and fines if they didn't plead guilty. In other words, they didn't seem to be genuinely sorry as much as they were trying to mitigate the penalty of paying for what they did wrong.

You can imagine the comments people have made—that the jail time wasn't enough (two months for Loughlin and five months for Giannulli), the fines weren't enough ($150,000 for Loughlin and $250,000 for Giannulli), and that neither is truly sorry for what they did. Let's just take it back to the fact that Felicity Huffman and Lori Loughlin had two very different approaches when it came to being contrite about what they had done. Huffman owned it, was truly sorry, served her time, and has put it all behind her now. Loughlin didn't own it, wasn't sorry, fought the case until continuing to do so would have been even more costly, and won't ever be able to put it behind her.

Any of us without sin need to cast the first stone on this one. Even though both actresses acted badly, one being contrite and the other not, I have compassion for both of them and won't be throwing any stones. I'm certainly thankful that none of my major moral misfires have been made known to the public, much less the wrong things I've done that I wasn't sorry about. Huffman and Loughlin have certainly paid a stiff price for being part of the Varsity Blues scandal. If we're honest, we can all identify with having a lack of contrition about our sins.

Developing a Contrite Attitude

If you are trying to be more of a rule-obeying, norm-complying, and tender-hearted person about how your misdeeds hurt others, here are some ideas on how to develop a contrite attitude in life. I hope they help you in your efforts to develop a contrite heart.

Own Your Mistakes. Don't blame others for your selfish and hurtful actions. Even if you had a gun to your head when you did them, you're still on the hook for the choices you make in life. The good, bad, and ugly ones. Stop blaming others for how you act.

Focus on How the Person You've Hurt Feels. Yep, we're back to compassion and empathy again. Far too often, people who do hurtful things only feel their emotional pain about it. "Oh, I feel so horrible about what I did!" That's not healthy sorrow. It's evidence that you are not contrite yet. Until you walk in the offended person's shoes and feel the pain they feel about what you did, you're not contrite.

Make Amends. Genuine sorrow over hurting others goes hand in hand with fixing what you broke. If you say, "I'm sorry for always being late" but don't start arriving on time, you aren't really sorry. If you say, "I'm sorry I called you an idiot" but don't stop calling a person an idiot, you aren't really sorry. Whatever damage you cause by your actions, you have to repair it by making amends. No amends, no sorrow.

Repair What You Did for the Other Person's Benefit, Not Your Own. Forgive me if I sound down on us human beings, but it strikes me that a lot of the time when people repair the damage they caused by their misdeeds they are doing it for themselves and not the offended person. In other words, we often make amends for what we did wrong because we want to quit feeling bad about having done it. If we are going to be contrite, we have to make amends for the sole purpose of leaving the other person better off, not ourselves.

See If You are Trending Toward Changing Your Ways. One of the best ways to assess if you are truly sorry about your hurtful actions is to see if your behavior is improving over time. If you aren't improving when it comes to doing the hurtful behavior less and less as time goes on, you aren't truly sorry. True sorrow over making mistakes shows up in the form of true change as you live your life. Everything else is just smoke and mirrors.

If you're like me, these were some painful tips to read. Far too often in my own life, I can see how I wanted to *appear* sorry for hurting others but really hadn't experienced being truly contrite about what I did. How do I know? The wrong behavior kept happening. I don't want us to beat ourselves up about all this, but I don't want us cutting ourselves too much slack here either. When you mess up and hurt another human being, I highly recommend that you practice these five tips.

Some Final Thoughts

I'm just as human and fallen as Felicity Huffman and Lori Laughlin will ever be. So are you. I say all this as someone who has worked with people long enough to know that the real issue in life isn't "Are we going to mess up?" That's a given. The real issue in life is "Are we going to be genuinely sorry and make amends when we mess up?" American historical novelist Sharon Kay Penman put it this way: "Men are born to sin . . . What does matter most, is not that we err, it is that we do benefit from our mistakes, that we are capable of sincere repentance, of genuine contrition."

I hope the vast majority of us will keep working to be the kind of people who are genuinely contrite when we mess up. Plutarch observed the wonderful things we have waiting for us if we are genuinely contrite when we make mistakes, saying, "Nothing can produce so great a serenity of life as a mind free from guilt and kept untainted, not only from actions, but purposes that are wicked. By this means the soul will be not only unpolluted but also undisturbed. The fountain will run clear and unsullied."

Do you want serenity? Do you want a mind free from toxic guilt? Do you want a mind untainted by purposes that are wicked? Do you want a soul that is unpolluted and undisturbed? Do you want a fountain coming out of you that is clear and unsullied? If you do, own your mistakes, have empathy for how they hurt others, make amends for their benefit, and make sure that you are trending in the direction of treating others better over time.

Let's work harder to avoid being a Fonzie in how we treat others so that it becomes easier over time to say we're sorry and really mean it.

Think About It

1. What unethical or immoral things have you done about which you had little, if any, contrition?

2. What unethical or immoral things have you done that you were contrite about and how did being genuinely sorry show up in terms of making amends to the person you hurt?

3. What did it feel like when someone who hurt you wasn't genuinely sorry? What did it feel like when someone who hurt you was genuinely sorry?

Chapter 19

Stand Up to Goliath: A Courageous Attitude

> I learned that courage was not the absence of fear, but the triumph over it. The brave man is not he who does not feel afraid, but he who conquers that fear.
>
> —Nelson Mandela

> So be strong and courageous, all you who put your hope in the Lord!
>
> —Psalm 31:24 (NLT)

It seems to me that most of the time when people talk about courage they are talking about courage on the battlefield. I've never experienced battle, at least not the war kind, and, to be honest, I don't know how I would handle it if my life and the lives of my fellow soldiers were on the line in combat. Would I be like Captain Miller in the movie *Saving Private Ryan*, who courageously led his men to storm the beaches at Normandy on D-Day, or like Corporal Upham, one of Captain Miller's men, who allowed fear to overcome him, something that contributed to the death of one of his fellow soldiers? I honestly don't know.

I want to talk about a different kind of courage in this chapter, moral courage. Moral courage is the willingness to stand up for what is right, just, and true. Chinese philosopher Confucius said, "To know what is the right thing to do and not do it is the greatest cowardice." Scottish novelist John Buchan said, "To see what is right and not to do it is cowardice. It is never a question of who is right but what is right." I don't know about you, but I find moral courage the hardest kind of courage to have in life.

We all struggle with some degree of cowardice in situations that involve physical danger, but I wonder if we don't struggle even more with cowardice when it comes to moral danger, the kind of danger that tests our conscience and our willingness to stand up against what is wrong. Let me give you one small example of a person who initially responded out of fear to a morally difficult situation but then found the courage to stand up and do what was right.

Refusing to Go to the Back of the Bus

A city ordinance was passed in 1900 in Montgomery, Alabama, to segregate bus passengers by race. The first four rows of the bus were set aside for whites and the remainder of the seats were set aside for blacks, who comprised seventy-five percent of the ridership. "Colored people" could sit in the middle rows until the bus filled up with whites. Once it filled up with whites, blacks were told to move to the back of the bus. If whites already filled the seats up front, blacks had to enter the door at the front of the bus to pay their fare, exit the bus, and re-enter it by the door in the back.

Enter Rosa Parks. Parks had ridden segregated buses in Montgomery for years. In her biography, she reported an incident in 1943 where she was attempting to board a bus through the front door because the back door was too crowded. The driver told her she had to get off the bus, board via the back door, and started to push her off the bus. Understandably not liking how the bigoted bus driver was treating her, Rosa made it clear she would leave on her own. Before doing so, she intentionally dropped her purse on the way out, sitting in a "white" seat as she picked it up. As she got off the bus to go to the back, the driver drove away leaving her stranded. Park's refused to ride this driver's bus for the next twelve years, choosing to walk many miles instead of allowing him to treat her in such a demeaning manner.

Fast forward twelve years. Parks decided to ride this driver's bus again. She was sitting in a middle row right behind the section reserved for whites, and more whites boarded the bus than there were available seats in the white section. The bus driver told Parks to give up her seat to the whites who were standing and go to the back of the bus. She initially refused and the bus driver threatened to have her arrested. The driver asked Parks if she was going to comply with his request. Her courageous response, "No, I'm not," led to her arrest. She was found guilty of violating a local ordinance (even though she was sitting in a seat designated for blacks) and fined $10 and $4 in court costs. Her act of defiance led the United States Congress to call her "the first lady of civil rights" and "the mother of the freedom movement."

In an interview on National Public Radio in 1992, Parks was asked what was behind her act of defiance. Parks's answer reflected her transformation from someone who allowed fear and conforming to social norms to control her to a courageous fighter for civil rights:

> I did not want to be mistreated, I did not want to be deprived of a seat that I had paid for. It was just time . . . there was opportunity for me to take a stand to express the way I felt about being treated in that manner. I had not planned to get arrested. I had plenty to do without having to end up in jail. But when I had to face that decision, I didn't hesitate to do so because I felt that we had endured that too long. The more we gave in, the more we complied with that kind of treatment, the more oppressive it became.

Again, I have no idea how I would have responded in that circumstance to racism in Montgomery in 1955 if I were black. I would like to think I would have had Rosa Parks's courage, that I would have been willing to face the ire of white people on the bus that day, get arrested, pay an unwarranted fine, and end up with a police record just to not give a white person my seat on the bus. Hard to say.

Psychologist Rollo May said, "The opposite of courage in our society is not cowardice, it is conformity." Parks decided to not conform that day in 1955, and, consequently, chose to be courageous. She, along with so many others involved in the civil rights movement, ratcheted up their efforts to oppose the evil of racism in society.

Sadly, too many people of color in our day and age are still having to show the same courage when it comes to resisting racism. We haven't come nearly as far as we might think, but, hopefully, we are making progress in our effort to combat the darker things about human nature that are so grossly flawed—racism, sexism, misogyny, xenophobia, and the like. Let's keep fighting the good fight when it comes to opposing these evils in our world.

Developing a Courageous Attitude

We all want to be courageous, to stand up to injustice and stand up for what it is right and fair. Yet, so many of us struggle to do so because of the price we might have to pay. Here are some tips for you just in case you might want to push the envelope on having more courage in your day-to-day life. Give these a try and see if you might not leave mankind better off and get some self-respect back.

Start with Something Small. Rather than wait until you are asked to storm a machine gun nest or refuse to go to the back of the bus, see if there might not be a smaller act of courage you could start with. For example, stand up against the smaller injustices at work that you notice, like the boss allowing his or her favorites to get to work late, leave early, or get the best projects. Each day offers us the chance to act courageously, even if it is relatively small and doesn't change human history.

Try Not to Worry About the Cost of Your Courage. If we pencil-whip the pros and cons of acting courageously, we'll pretty much talk ourselves out of doing the right thing. Far too often, the cons of acting courageously far outweigh the pros, and you have to be willing to accept that and not allow it to dissuade you from doing what you know is proper. Doing the right thing will often have a big price tag that goes along with it, but acting that way leaves the world better off and allows you to hang on to your self-respect.

Leave Punishment Up to God or Karma. As a theist, I believe God is ultimately going to judge everyone's actions and justly reward or punish people accordingly. That is why right-minded theists don't presume to take revenge in their own hands. If you aren't a theist, then I guess you have to trust Karma and assume that what goes around comes around in life. Whatever worldview you have, please don't take revenge in your own hands.

Act in Spite of Your Fears. We've heard this from a zillion different people, that courage is not the absence of fear but acting in spite of your fears. As we saw at the top of this chapter, Nelson Mandela said, "I learned that courage was not the absence of fear, but the triumph over it. The brave man is not he who does not feel afraid, but he who conquers that fear." That's coming from someone who triumphed over his fears time and time again in fighting apartheid in South Africa. Easier said than done, but the challenge here is to not let your fears control you. Piers Anthony put it this way: "Being terrified but going ahead and doing what must be done—that's courage. The one who feels no fear is a fool, and the one who lets fear rule him is a coward."

Persevere. A single act of courage is fine, but we need to act courageously time and time again. Ralph Waldo Emerson said, "A hero is no braver than an ordinary man, but he is braver five minutes longer." My dad, God rest his soul, was a navigator-bombardier in World War II. With each new dawn, he had to decide to be courageous again and again in order to board a B-24 bomber and fly incredibly dangerous missions over Europe. I admire that about him—that he wasn't just courageous once but over and over. He persevered in being courageous, and, along with the other men and women who served, left the world a better place.

If you're like me, courage is something you want the other guy or gal to have when it comes time to stand up to evil. Yet, somehow, we need to find it in ourselves and be willing to take great risks in the face of the immoral things that happen each day. Courage lives inside each of us; we just have to be willing to express it. When we're the ones told to get to the back of the bus, we've got to find our inner Rosa Parks and be willing to courageously fight back, even if we pay a high price.

Some Final Thoughts

A cowardly attitude is extremely destructive, whether it is on a literal battlefield or the moral battlefield. Far too often in politics, we see people unwilling to show courage in the positions they take or the votes they make once in office because it might lead to them not getting elected, losing their seat in Congress, or experiencing the wrath of people in their own party. Some people wait until they are about to leave office to "vote their conscience," not something that is truly courageous at all.

We admire the people who have the courage to stand up against evil and risk everything in the process. William Shakespeare said, "Cowards die many times before their deaths; the valiant never taste of death but once." He's got that right. If you're like me, you have exhibited moral cowardice on more than a few occasions, keeping silent when you needed to stand up and make your voice heard. Very rarely are we asked to put our physical lives on the line, but we get asked fairly often to put our moral lives on the line and stand up for what is right, fair, and true. When we fail to be courageous about standing up for the good and against the bad, we die before our death.

Sure, you're going to find out how courageous you are on the battlefield, but you're also going to find out how courageous you are on a segregated bus in Montgomery, Alabama, in the 1950s. Chuck Swindoll observed, "Courage is not limited to the battlefield or the Indianapolis 500 or bravely catching a thief in your house. The real tests of courage are much quieter. They are the inner tests, like remaining faithful when nobody's looking, like enduring pain when the room is empty, like standing alone when you're misunderstood."

How's your inner Rosa Parks these days? Are you ready, willing, and able to make your voice heard in opposing evil? If you are, you'll only die once.

Think About It

1. Without rubbing your own nose in it, where have you failed to muster the courage necessary for standing up against evil?

2. Where have you found the courage to stand up for what is right, fair, and true?

3. Who have you seen show moral courage and how did he or she show it? Who have you seen show moral cowardice and how did he or she show it?

Chapter 20

Nurse Their Wounds: A Caring Attitude

To be successful is to be helpful, caring and constructive, to make
everything and everyone you touch a little bit better.

—Norman Vincent Peale

Do nothing out of selfish ambition or vain conceit. Rather, in humility
value others above yourselves, not looking to your own interests but
each of you to the interests of the others.

—Philippians 2:3-4

I'm so proud of my kids I could bust my buttons. The reason I'm proud of
them is not because of how much they have accomplished academically
and professionally, even though they have accomplished a great deal. The
reason I'm proud of them is because of how much they care about people.

My son, Matt, has cared about people by becoming a lawyer and being
a public defender for a number of years. My middle daughter, Ashley, has
cared about people by being a psychologist and helping them deal with
difficult emotional and relational problems. And, my youngest daughter,
Kelly, has cared about people by being a nurse. They have all lived their lives
by Quaker missionary Stephen Grellet's famous saying, "I expect to pass
through life but once. If therefore, there be any kindness I can show, or any
good thing I can do to any fellow being, let me do it now, and not defer or
neglect it, as I shall not pass this way again." Did I tell you I'm so proud of
my kids I could bust my buttons?

For the purpose of this chapter, I want to zero in on someone in the field my youngest daughter is in, a woman who epitomized being a caring individual. Before I do, I want to say that in the midst of the coronavirus pandemic, I recently got a picture from Kelly at the hospital where she works in New York City, the epicenter of the coronavirus at the time I write these words.

Kelly and the other nurses were covered in protective garb, courageously caring for all the little ones in the NICU (neonatal intensive care unit) who were holding on for dear life. The hospital Kelly works for has close to 800 beds, and the majority of them were occupied by patients infected with the COVID-19 when she sent me the picture. I want to give a well-deserved shout out to all the health professionals and first responders around the country who have been putting their lives on the line each day by fighting the good fight against this horrible virus. Every one of them are heroes. No one had to teach these amazing people how to be caring or courageous. They just are. We owe them a huge debt of gratitude, now and in the years to come.

Angel of the Battlefield

Clara Barton was born on Christmas Day, 1821. When Barton was ten, she took on the task of nursing her brother, David, back to health after he suffered a severe head injury falling off the roof of a barn. An overly shy and timid person, her parents pushed her to become a schoolteacher. She earned her teacher's certificate at the age of seventeen and her competence as a teacher helped her confidence to grow.

After her mother's death, Barton furthered her education by attending college. She continued to be so effective as a teacher that she was contracted to open up a school in a nearby town. Her efforts were so successful that the town felt compelled the to raise $4,000 for a new school building. Apparently, misogyny was alive and well at the time, because the school board elected a male to be the principal of the new school rather than Barton. They didn't feel such a large and important institution should be headed by a woman.

Barton moved to Washington, D.C. in 1855 to work as a patent clerk in the US Patent Office, the first time a woman had received a significant clerkship in the federal government at a salary equal to a man. Many of the causalities of the early days of the Civil War were sent to Washington. Desiring to serve her country, Barton went to the train station where the causalities arrived and provided clothing, food, and supplies for the sick and wounded soldiers. She provided emotional support for the soldiers by reading to them, writing letters to their families, and encouraging them. During that time, Barton committed to working with the Army as a nurse and used her own living quarters as a storeroom for medical supplies.

In 1862, Barton gained permission to work on the front lines during the Civil War. She worked tirelessly to distribute supplies, apply dressings, clean field hospitals, and serve food to wounded soldiers, helping both Union and Confederate casualties. She was appointed "lady in charge" of the hospitals at the front lines of the war and became known as the "Florence Nightingale of America," a high honor given that Florence Nightingale is credited with being the founder of modern nursing. She was also known as the "Angel of the Battlefield." If you saw the movie *Dances with Wolves*, you don't need me to describe how much unimaginable pain and suffering occurred in the field hospitals where Barton worked.

At the end of the Civil War, Barton discovered thousands of letters from distraught relatives to the War Department that had gone unanswered concerning their missing loved ones. She was given permission by President Lincoln to officially respond to these letters and was named superintendent of the Office of Missing Soldiers. Barton and her associates wrote 41,855 replies and helped to locate more than 22,000 men who were missing. She spent the summer of 1865 finding, identifying, and properly burying 13,000 men who had died in a Confederate prisoner of war camp.

Barton delivered lectures around the country about her experiences during the Civil War and achieved national recognition. She closed the Office of Missing Soldiers in 1868 and was so mentally and physically exhausted that her doctor ordered her to get away from her work to regain her health. While on a trip to Geneva, Switzerland, Barton was introduced to the International Red Cross and was asked by its leader to be the representative of the American Branch of the Red Cross. Barton came back to the United States and founded the American Red Cross in 1881, at the age of fifty-nine, and subsequently led it for twenty-three years. As if she had not done enough, after she resigned from the leadership of the American Red Cross, Barton founded the National First Aid Society, which was aimed at promoting local first aid programs. She served as its national honorary president for five years.

I don't know about you, but, when I compare my life to the life of Clara Barton, I feel humbled. From a very early age, she devoted her life to caring for others, nursing them back to health. If Norman Vincent Peale is right, that to be successful is to be "helpful, caring, and constructive," then may I offer you Clara Barton as one of the most successful Americans who ever lived. She set the standard for having a caring heart, something backed up by decades of sacrificial and selfless service. I think I'm going to quit talking myself out of holding doors open for people, letting them into traffic, or bringing meals over when someone is sick. I'm going to blame Clara Barton for that.

Stephen Grellet is telling it like it is when he says that we only pass through life once and that any act of caring and kindness on our part toward our fellow human beings is to be done now and not deferred. In a world that seems to be full of people who are only "looking out for number one," it's the least we can do. Martin Luther King, Jr. echoed this when he said, "Life's most persistent and urgent question is, 'What are you doing for others?'" That's the question that needs to challenge us every day, don't you think?

Developing a Caring Attitude

Caring about the needs of others is non-negotiable if you want to call yourself a human being. If you don't care much or at all about the troubled and downtrodden, you're more of a human doing than a human being. Here are some tips for how to develop a caring attitude as you go through life.

Look Around and Identify Needs. Sometimes, because we're thinking about ourselves too much, we don't look around and see how many needs there are in the world that we could meet. Too focused on our own neediness, we keep our head down, ruminate about what we don't have, and live self-centered lives. Take time each day to take a look around and see if there are needs that jump out at you, and do what you can to meet them.

Act. When you see a need that you can meet, meet it. Good intentions don't mean much in life. Remember the proverb, "The road to hell is paved with good intentions"? That is so true. Get off your good intentions and act on them. What good does it do you or anyone else to say "I meant to help that little old lady across the street before she got hit by a car" if you didn't help her? Do everything you can to keep from saying, "I intended to." Remember what Yoda told Luke Skywalker in *Star Wars*, "Do. Or do not. There is no try."

Be Careful. There are people out there who are good at exploiting others. I got cornered one time at a convenience store by a woman who came in crying, walked up to me and told me her sob story, and said she needed gas money to get to a doctor's appointment. I gave her ten dollars. She promptly got into a late model car with a man who had a six-pack of beer with him and drove off. There are people in genuine need, but she wasn't one of them. There are devious people who have spent their lives being irresponsible, selfish, and exploitive of tender-hearted folks. After that happened, I made a decision to never give money to someone unless I knew where the money was going. Consequently, I only give money to reputable organizations that have a history of putting contributions to good use.

Keep in Mind How Some People Have It Much Worse Than You. Don't lose sight of how good you've got it in life (assuming that you do). It breaks my heart when I hear some of the struggles people have, and I thank God for how good my life is compared to what others are going through. You can tell a culture's heart by how it looks out for the poor, the oppressed, the sick, and the widowed. For many of these people, each day is a difficult struggle and they desperately need our help.

Volunteer. Find a cause you are passionate about and join with others in serving that group of people. When we pool our time, talents, and treasures together in the service of needy people, a lot of good can happen. I have a friend who has volunteered for years to serve in a soup kitchen to feed the poor. He doesn't have any more time on his hands than I do, but he puts it to good use every Saturday morning in a way that positively benefits those who are destitute and hungry. I admire that about him.

There are hundreds of other ways to care about people. I hope these tips were helpful to you and will motivate you to express your care for others.

Some Final Thoughts

Former First Lady Rosalyn Carter reminds us of something very important about the issue of being caring. She said, "There are only four kinds of people in the world—those who have been caregivers, those who are caregivers, those who will be caregivers and those who will need caregivers." When we are no longer able to actively care about others, whether it be because of illness or old age, we need to be able to look back at our lives and say that we have been all four kinds of people. If we can't, our lives were probably not much of a success.

Mother Teresa said, "At the end of life we will not be judged by how many diplomas we have received, how much money we have made, how many great things we have done. We will be judged by 'I was hungry, and you gave me something to eat, I was naked and you clothed me. I was homeless, and you took me in.'" Let's keep moving in that direction.

Think About It

1. Think back to the last time someone caringly and sacrificially reached out to help you. What was that like and how did it feel?

2. Who in your life do you need to treat in a more caring manner?

3. Who do you need to allow to care for you? How can they care for you?

Chapter 21

Believe You Can If You Can:
A Confident Attitude

Each time we face our fear, we gain strength, courage, and confidence in the doing.

—Theodore Roosevelt

So we say with confidence, "The Lord is my helper; I will not be afraid. What can mere mortals do to me?"

—Hebrews 13:6

I am horribly afraid of heights. I mean horribly. When my wife, Holly, and I went to see the Grand Canyon a number of years ago, it was not a pleasant experience for me. I stood back as far as I could from the edge of the canyon, almost to the point of not being able to look down into it. I probably should have just watched a nice documentary on the dang thing rather than drive all the way out to Arizona only to want to leave as soon as I arrived.

Not only am I deathly afraid of heights, I'm deathly afraid of heights *for others*. When I went to the Grand Canyon, I was just as afraid for the other tourists as I was for myself. I found myself getting incredibly anxious as I watched people go up to the edge to get a panoramic view of this geological masterpiece.

I must admit that I also felt some anger toward some of the tourists for causing me to have a panic attack by not being as careful as they needed to be. I wanted to scold them after they walked away from the edge with "What the heck is wrong with you? Are you brain dead? You're a complete idiot to have gotten that close to the edge!" All this was confirmed recently when I read that a number of people had fallen to their death while taking a selfie at the edge of the canyon. My heart broke, but I also felt angry that people wouldn't be more careful.

While this might sound like a chapter on the importance of a courageous attitude in life, it isn't. We've already covered that in a previous chapter when we talked about Rosa Parks having the courage to stand up to racism in the deep South in the 1950s by refusing to go to the back of the bus. Here, I want to talk about the importance of a confident attitude in life.

In this chapter, I'm going to talk about *appropriate* confidence, not *foolhardy* confidence. We live in a time when people are often told by motivational speakers, "You can do anything you set your mind to." That's not true, and it only emboldens people to take foolish risks that come back to bite them in some painful and even deadly ways. With that in mind, let me introduce you to the world's most confident rock climber.

You Did What? Are You Nuts?

I saw an amazing documentary recently, *Free Solo*. It won the Academy Award for Best Documentary Feature in 2019. *Free Solo* is about 33-year old Alex Hannold's almost decade long quest to climb El Capitan, 3,000 feet of vertical rock in Yosemite Park. Hannold wasn't determined to simply climb El Capitan the way others have, with ropes and anchors. He was determined to climb it *without a rope*! Let me say that again. Hannold was determined to climb one of the toughest rock formations in the world *without a rope*!

Now, when I go out into my yard with my twelve-foot extension ladder to clean my rain gutters, I don't even feel comfortable climbing up on it. This guy wanted to climb the sheer face of a 3,000-foot wall of rock *without a rope*. *Free Solo* goes into Hannold's background, how he was drawn to rock climbing from an early age, that he was a very shy and reserved kid prone to depression growing up, and how climbing helped him to develop a more positive sense of himself and gain more confidence. *Free Solo* also lets the viewer in on Hannold's unhealthy pursuit of perfection, his inability to feel emotions like the average person does, how his aspirations put significant stress on all the people around him, and how his rock-climbing aspirations were more important than intimate relationships with others.

I say all this to get to the main point of the chapter. To do anything that's difficult or challenging in life, you have to have a confident attitude. Hannold certainly did, but *Free Solo* helped to unlock why he would be confident about doing something that very few, if any, world-class rock climbers would even attempt. Hannold's confidence was born out of some very important things that I want you to keep in mind as you listen to people like me tell you to need a confident attitude in life.

First, Hannold was drawn from childhood to climbing rocks. It was something he was meant to do. As Marie Curie put it, "We must believe that we are gifted for something, and that this thing, at whatever cost, must be attained." When it comes to performing difficult and complex tasks, you have to have a fairly high level of natural ability and talent to be able to do them well. Let me put this a different way—it is foolish to be confident that you can perform at a high level if you don't have the wiring, talent, and ability to do so.

Second, Hannold prepared to the max. He didn't just think to himself one day, "Hey, I think I'll climb El Capitan—it ought to be a piece of cake." Hannold trained his mind and body over a period of years to rock climb such that he was able to control his innate fear response. Hannold climbed El Capitan roughly fifty times *roped-up* in the years before he free soloed, getting in better shape and figuring out every nook-and-cranny of how he was going to climb it. Former Dallas Cowboy Roger Staubach said "Confidence doesn't come out of nowhere. It's a result of something . . . hours and days and weeks and years of constant work and dedication." Part of Hannold's confidence was that he had spent so much time preparing that the actual climb was just the fruit of his intense labor.

Third, Hannold minimized the risks of the climb as best he could. Given that he was climbing without a rope, Hannold knew he couldn't completely eliminate the risk of falling. But, his talent at rock climbing, the way his mind interpreted fear, the level of preparation, and choosing to climb on a good-weather day were some of the wise ways he minimized the risk of falling. Another thing he did to lessen the risk of falling was that with fellow climber, Conrad Anker, he went 1500 feet up the face of El Capitan prior to the climb and removed all the rocks that could come loose during his free solo effort.

Finally, Hannold was wise enough to know when climbing El Capitan was a no-go. He did not make it to the top during his first try. On that day, Hannold got a few hundred feet up the face of El Capitan before he turned back to the valley floor. From how the documentary portrayed it, he felt that wasn't the day it was going to work out for him to climb El Capitan, and he wisely postponed his accomplishment by seven months, possibly saving his life.

There is a huge difference between wise confidence and foolish confidence. Some motivational speakers will tell you that "You can do anything you set your mind to" in an effort to instill confidence in you. Given the finiteness and limitations of each human being, *there is absolutely no way in the world that you can do anything you set your mind to, and you are experiencing foolish confidence if you think you can.*

Walt Disney said, "The four Cs of making dreams come true: Curiosity, Courage, Consistency, Confidence." Alex Hannold had all four the day he free soloed El Capitan. He had spent years being curious about making the climb, had the courage necessary to attempt it, consistently prepared to the fullest degree he could, and, in light of these three, had the confidence he could do it. It was truly an amazing feat by an amazing individual in this particular area of expertise.

By the way, I'm never going to watch *Free Solo* again. Even though I know Hannold makes it to the top safely, it still sends a shiver up my spine to watch what he did. I'm happy for him, but I hope he won't do anything like that again.

Developing a Confident Attitude

In this section on tips for developing a confident attitude, I'm going to go back to what I've already said about Hannold free-soloing El Capitan. I do this because any other tips would be a waste of time, and I don't want to do that to you. So, here are some important tips for developing a confident attitude.

Make Sure You Have the Necessary Talent and Ability. Don't buy into the idea that you can do anything you set your mind to. If you want to be confident about something, make sure you have the ability to do it. If you want to be a confident tennis player, make sure you can walk and chew gum at the same time. If you want to be a confident piano player, make sure you aren't all thumbs. Confidence without the talent and ability to back it up is foolish.

Train. Don't cut corners when it comes to putting in the proper amount of preparation to achieve things in life. Far too many of us don't want to put enough sweat equity into achieving things. To go back to my tennis analogy, too many people show up on the day of a match not having put in enough time on the practice court hitting ball after ball in the hot sun. Don't be lazy when it comes to preparing for a performance. If you haven't worked hard to get ready, confidence that you're going to succeed is probably misplaced.

Reduce the Risks. Do whatever you can to reduce or eliminate things that could get in the way of performing well. You don't want to attempt something with anything nagging you in the back of your mind about it. Back to tennis again, if you are worried about the racquet slipping in your hand, put some absorbent tape on the grip. If you are worried about rolling your ankle because it is weak, tape it up. If you are worried about the sun being in your eyes, wear sunglasses or a visor. Eliminate everything you can (other than your opponent) that will distract you or pose a risk to accomplishing your goal.

Know When It's a No-Go. There are days when your efforts aren't likely to work out. I think we still ought to step out on the court and give it a try, but, if after a few games you pass out from dehydration, roll your ankle, or get hit in the face with an overhead that makes it impossible to see, you need to accept the fact that today may not be the day you are going to succeed. We walk a fine line here. Some people give up prematurely when they could have actually succeeded at accomplishing something. But the other mistake we make is not knowing when to admit defeat and live to fight another day.

Don't Let Confidence Turn into Cockiness. Some people allow success at a given endeavor to turn into arrogance and cockiness. They think being able to do something well makes them a better human being than everyone else and forget where their talent and ability came from (God). They get too full of themselves and their confidence turns into becoming an insufferable human being. Hall of Fame quarterback Johnny Unitas said, "There is a difference between conceit and confidence. Conceit is bragging about yourself. Confidence means you believe you can get the job done." Confidence in a given area of life, absolutely! Cockiness in any area of life, God forbid.

I hope all this helps. Alex Hannold had the talent to climb El Capitan, prepared adequately, reduced the risks, knew when it wasn't going to happen, and was confident but never cocky. All of that came together and is why he succeeded in accomplishing something that we mere mortals would never even try.

A final way to put this is to quote one of the most famous verses in the Bible, "Pride goes before destruction, a haughty spirit before a fall" (Proverbs 16:18). When we get too full of ourselves and try to do things we are not the least bit ready, willing, or able to do, we are going to experience a painful and destructive fall. We would all be wise to remember that before we presume to tackle our own version of El Capitan.

Some Final Thoughts

We live in a weird world when it comes to the issue of having a confident attitude. Far too many motivational speakers try to instill confidence in their audience, but I sometimes wonder if they aren't destructively instilling confidence that certain audience members shouldn't have. I'm all for encouraging people to work on turning deficits into strengths so they can accomplish more than they thought possible, but success is still going to come down to the big five—having the ability, training, reducing the risks, knowing when it isn't going to happen, and avoiding any hint of cockiness.

If you are a parent, I want to caution you about something. Don't try to instill confidence in your children that they shouldn't have. Don't tell your child what so many parents tell theirs, "You can do anything you set your mind to." That's simply not true. If your child isn't drawn to science and is average in intelligence, don't encourage them that they could be a nuclear physicist someday. But, don't make the opposite mistake either. If your child is musically oriented and seems to have talent when it comes to singing or playing an instrument, encourage them to see how far their talent and hard work can take them in that area. Then, get out of their way and see how well they do against the competition.

You know by now that I'm a golf nut. Widely considered to be the greatest golfer of all time (I think it's Tiger Woods), Jack Nicklaus offers us the following wisdom, "Confidence is the most important single factor in this game, and no matter how great your natural talent, there is only one way to obtain and sustain it: work." What Nicklaus said applies to life more broadly—confidence is one of the most important things you can have in life but it needs to be grounded in reality and a reflection of all the hard work you have done to excel at a given endeavor.

Think About It

1. Where in your life did you act on foolish confidence in attempting to do something, and how did that turn out for you?

2. What have you not attempted to do in life because you lacked the confidence you actually should have had?

3. Where have you seen both of the above in the people you love and how might you help them see the truth?

Chapter 22

Do the Right Thing:
A Conscientious Attitude

> I leave comparisons to history, claiming only that I have acted in every instance from a conscientious desire to do what was right, constitutional, within the law, and for the very best interests of the whole people. Failures have been errors of judgment, not of intent.
>
> —Ulysses S. Grant

> So I strive always to keep my conscience clear before God and man.
>
> —Acts 24:16

M ultiple times each day, we stand at the fork in the road between doing what is right and doing what is wrong. Those whose consciences are fairly seared will often opt for the road of doing what is wrong because it feels better in the moment and brings about the most immediate reward or payoff. Those whose consciences are alive and well, more often than not, opt for the path of doing what is right even if it involves a painful personal cost.

I'm about to share with you one of the many reasons why I will never be elected president of the United States. The reason it will never happen is that my slogan wouldn't have been "Make America Great Again" (MAGA), it would have been "Make America Moral Again" (MAMA). Who is going to vote for someone whose campaign slogan is MAMA?

Another reason I will never be elected president is that I believe in the death penalty for people who ride my bumper.

With that in mind, allow me to introduce you to the kind of person we need to model our lives after, someone who had a conscientious attitude in the two different ways the word is defined. *The Free Dictionary* says that conscientious means both "guided by or in accordance with the dictates of conscience" and "thorough and assiduous." This man was both—guided by his conscience and thorough and hard-working in his efforts.

I don't hold any human being up as a Christ-figure because no one comes anywhere close. Nevertheless, this person set a pretty high bar for we mere mortals and is an inspiration to those of us who strive to allow our conscience be our guide and work hard at what we do.

The Straightest of Arrows

He was born August 7, 1944, and grew up in Princeton, New Jersey, before his family moved to Philadelphia. He earned an undergraduate degree in political science at Princeton University and a master's degree in international relations from New York University. The death of a classmate in the Vietnam War led him to enlist in the Marines. He entered Officer Candidate Training and graduated from Army Ranger school and Army jump school. He was sent to Vietnam in 1968 and served as a platoon leader. His military decorations and awards include: the Bronze Star Medal with Combat "V," the Purple Heart Medal, two Navy and Marine Corps Commendation Medals with Combat "V," Combat Action Ribbon, National Defense Service Medal, Vietnam Service Medal with four service stars, Republic of Vietnam Gallantry Cross, Republic of Vietnam Campaign Medal, and Parachutist Badge.

After leaving the Marines, he graduated from the University of Virginia Law School and worked as a litigator in a law firm before serving twelve years in the United States Attorney offices in San Francisco and Boston, where he prosecuted terrorism and public corruption cases, financial fraud, narcotics conspiracies, and international money launderers. He served as a partner in a Boston law firm before returning to government service in the United States Department of Justice. He became the United States Assistant Attorney General in charge of the Department of Justice Criminal Division. He was later named US Attorney for the Northern District of California, a position he held for three years.

President George W. Bush tabbed him to be the director of the FBI in 2001, and he was *unanimously* confirmed by the Senate one week before the September 11 attacks on the World Trade Center and the Pentagon. He served as FBI director with distinction and was asked by President Barack Obama to extend his stay at the FBI two additional years beyond the traditional ten-year limit. He returned to the private sector working in a law firm, teaching, consulting, and speaking.

On May 17, 2017, he was appointed by Deputy Attorney General Rod Rosenstein to serve as Special Counsel in the United States Department of Justice and investigate "any links and/or coordination between the Russian government and individuals associated with the campaign of President Donald Trump, and any matters that arose or may arise directly from the investigation." His appointment elicited widespread support from both Republicans and Democrats in Congress. He pulled together a "dream team" of lawyers and investigators, and his determination and hard work led to multiple felony convictions. On March 22nd, 2019, Robert Swan Mueller III turned in his final report to Attorney General William Barr regarding his investigation of Russian meddling in the 2016 presidential election and the degree to which anyone in Trump's inner circle conspired with them or participated in obstruction of justice.

Why am I telling you all this? I'm trying to hold up a particular person as the poster child for what it means to have a conscientious attitude and live a life of moral decency and integrity. Sure, Mueller is a human being with his flaws, but can you think of anyone else in this country who has lived his life in a way the Bible refers to as "above reproach" and "in a manner worthy of full respect" (1 Timothy 3:2, 4)?

Mueller reminds me of Atticus Finch in the movie *To Kill a Mockingbird*. You may remember that Atticus was tabbed by the local judge to defend a black man falsely accused of raping a white woman in Alabama in the 1930s. In this case, Atticus knew that his client, Tom Robinson, had not raped this white woman and that the racist influencers in town were falsely accusing him. Atticus conducted himself with impeccable moral integrity in trying the case even though Tom was ultimately judged to be guilty of the crime by an all-white jury. From my perspective, Mueller is our country's Atticus Finch.

Throughout American history, there have been men and women with a healthy conscience who have had the courage to take on the unenviable task of pursuing truth no matter where it might lead or what the cost of finding it might be. Mueller is that kind of person. We are fortunate to have someone whose integrity is above reproach and who fulfilled both aspects of what it means to be conscientious.

Mueller was both moral and thorough in how he conducted the Russia investigation and was the right person for the job. While some were critical he did not force Trump to testify in person to expose the lies he told during the investigation or publicly state the House of Representatives needed to move forward with articles of impeachment for obstruction of justice, Robert Swan Mueller III demonstrated a conscientious attitude by diligently pursuing the truth wherever it might lead.

Developing a Conscientious Attitude

How does one develop a conscientious attitude, one that will lead you to do the right thing with hard work and perseverance regardless of the cost is to your reputation or career? Here are some possibilities.

Be Clear About Right and Wrong. Some people have what we call "situational ethics," which means that their definition of right and wrong depends on the situation they find themselves in. It is important to tightly nail down what your ethics and morals are before a tough situation arises. Call me old-fashioned if you want to, but the world seems to be getting grayer about what is right and wrong, something that leads to people folding like a lawn chair when a moral dilemma hits them in the face.

Be Willing to Pay the Price for Standing Firm on Your Moral Convictions. If you are like me, you worry a tad too much about what people will think about you if you remain true to your moral code, especially when they vehemently disagree with you on a given issue. Even if someone tries to metaphorically nail you to a cross, don't cater or crater when it comes to living by your moral code. You never want to sacrifice your moral integrity just to please others or stay in someone's favor. Never play to the crowd when it comes to how you act morally.

Admit When You Violate Your Moral Code. We have already talked about the fact that we are human beings and make a lot of mistakes along the way. That's not the issue. The issue is to take responsibility when you do. Don't deny your mistake, don't blame it on someone else, don't focus on how others do the same thing, and don't justify it. *Own it!* Don't make excuses or rationalize your wrong actions. Be an adult who stands up and says, "What I did was wrong, it was my fault, I'm truly sorry, and here is how I'm going to make amends."

Don't Look Down Your Nose at Morally Fallen People. People who are healthy in owning their moral mistakes and being sorry when they mess up don't look down their nose at other "sinners." They remind themselves, "There but for the grace of God go I." It sounds paradoxical, but the more morally healthy you are the humbler you become. You and I are no better than anyone else *on the planet* morally regardless of whether or not we would ever do some of the immoral things others do.

Don't Shame or Condemn Yourself When You Violate Your Moral Code, and Don't let Others Shame or Condemn You Either. So many of us have a tendency to bring out the moral whopping stick when we mess up, shaming and condemning ourselves for our moral misfires. Don't do that. The moral mistakes you make are penalty enough in terms of how they damage your soul and hurt those around you. Offer yourself grace and compassion when you act immorally, not the self-indulgent kind that leads you to keep messing up but the "go and sin no more" kind that leads you to chart a better moral course.

There are so many other ways to develop a conscientious attitude. I hope these tips were helpful to you. The main point I'm trying to make is that we need to keep working on living lives that are above reproach, living morally in a way that would make it hard for someone to legitimately criticize our actions. That's how Robert Mueller appears to have lived his life and why he was tasked with perhaps the most important investigation in American history. Let's keep working on having a Robert Mueller attitude.

Some Final Thoughts

A healthy conscience is the one thing you can't afford to lose in life. You can lose your hair, your patience, and, on a bad day, your mind, but you simply cannot afford to lose a sense of right and wrong when it comes to how you live your life morally.

Let me throw a number of quotes at you to drive all this home. Benjamin Franklin said, "A good conscience is a continual Christmas." James Madison said, "Conscience is the most sacred of all property." Martin Luther

King, Jr. said, "I submit than an individual who breaks a law that conscience tells him is unjust, and who willingly accepts the penalty of imprisonment in order to arouse the conscience of the community over its injustice, is in reality expressing the highest respect for the law." Albert Einstein said, "Never do anything against conscience even if the state demands it." Blaise Pascal said, "If we regulate our conduct according to our own convictions, we may safely disregard the praise or censure of others." James Freeman Clarke said, "Conscience in the soul is the root of all true courage. If a man would be brave, let him learn to obey his conscience." And, finally, Michael Eric Dyson said, "I'm nervous about the prospects of an America that refuses to abide by its best conscience and its best lights and its best angels."

Every one of these people are saying something important. Unless we allow our God-wired conscience to be our guide, we will continue to harm ourselves, those around us, the country, and the world we live in.

I leave you with one final quote. English poet Joseph Addison said, "A good conscience is to the soul what health is to the body; it preserves constant ease and serenity within us; and more than countervails all the calamities and afflictions which can befall us from without." Let's aspire as individuals and as a country to go back to doing things because they are right to do so our consciences can grow stronger and our country can return to its former greatness as a place that puts its brightest lights and its best angels front and center.

Think About It

1. Without rubbing your own nose in it, what immoral thing have you done that was the most significant violation of your conscience?

2. Looking back in time, what is the greatest act of morality you have done that kept you at peace with your conscience?

3. What current situation are you facing where you are being tempted to violate your conscience and do the wrong thing?

Chapter 23

Be at Peace with Others:
A Conciliatory Attitude

> Anyone can love peace, but Jesus didn't say, "Blessed are the peace-lovers." He says peacemakers. He is referring to a life vocation, not a hobby on the sidelines of life.
>
> —Jim Wallis

> If it is possible, as far as it depends on you, live a peace with everyone.
>
> Romans 12:18

It's often said that there are two kind of people in the world, givers and takers. Given how complex, complicated, and nuanced we human beings are, this kind of simplistic label can't possibly be true and falls well short of understanding how unique we are as individuals. Nevertheless, I get what those who say this are trying to do—give us a shorthand for how to understand and deal with people.

At the risk of adding to the problem of simplistically labeling people, I want to suggest another category of human beings—troublemakers and peacemakers. Again, much too simplistic and shallow, but I think you know what I'm doing to suggest such an all-or-nothing view of people. Even though each of us is a unique mixture of both, we generally fall into the troublemaker or peacemaker category.

When it comes to the troublemakers, the police and our court system are supposed to deal with them. When it comes to the peacemakers, financial support, praise, and awards are meant to deal with them. For the peacemakers, there is one award above all others.

The Nobel Peace Prize, named after Alfred Nobel, the man who invented dynamite, has been awarded 100 times to 134 Nobel Laureates between 1901 and 2019. One-hundred-and-six individuals and twenty-seven organizations have won the prize, which is awarded annually to "who shall have done the most or the best work for fraternity between nations, for the abolition or reduction of standing armies and for the holding and promotion of peace congresses."

When a person receives the Nobel Peace Prize, he or she is being honored as a world-class peacemaker who has done a great deal to oppose world-class troublemakers and try to bring about as much peace in the world as possible.

Some famous people have won the Nobel Peace Prize, including Barack Obama, Jimmy Carter, Desmond Tutu, the fourteenth Dalai Lama, Mother Teresa, Henry Kissinger, Martin Luther King, Jr., Albert Schweitzer, and Theodore Roosevelt. Of all those who have won the Nobel Peace Prize, I want to highlight one individual who took peacemaking to a whole new level.

Freedom Fighting Peacemaker

Nelson Rolihlahla Mandela was born in Mvezo, South Africa, July 18, 1918, and died in Johannesburg, South Africa, December 5, 2013. His father was the chief of the Madiba clan of the Tembu people. After his father died, he renounced his claim to the chieftainship and became a lawyer. In 1944 he joined the African National Congress (ANC), a black liberation group. He established South Africa's first black law practice in Johannesburg in 1952 and specialized in cases resulting from 1948 apartheid legislation by the all-white leaders of the country. As you know, apartheid was South Africa's policy of segregating blacks from whites and enforcing political and economic discrimination.

Mandela launched a campaign against South Africa's "pass laws." These laws required blacks to carry documents, known as passes or pass books, authorizing their presence in areas the government deemed as "restricted," meaning areas that were reserved for whites. Mandela traveled South Africa trying to build support for nonviolent ways to end these laws.

In 1955, Mandela helped to draft the Freedom Charter, a document that called for non-racial democracy in South Africa.

Whether you are a troublemaker or peacemaker is in the eye of the beholder. Obviously, the authorities in South Africa saw Mandela as a troublemaker, and they severely restricted him in terms of travel, whom he could associate with, and the speeches he could give. After a massacre of unarmed black men by police in 1960, Mandela abandoned his non-violent stance against authorities and began to advocate for acts of sabotage against the South African regime. In 1963, Mandela was tried for treason, sabotage, and violent conspiracy. He was sentenced to life in prison and narrowly avoided the death penalty. His imprisonment was a cause celebre among the international community that was opposed to apartheid in South Africa.

Mandela was released from prison in 1990 after serving *twenty-six years* and was chosen deputy president of the African National Congress. He became the president of the party in 1991. Mandela worked with President de Klerk to end apartheid and bring about a peaceful transition to social democracy in South Africa. The two of them were awarded the Nobel Peace Prize in 1993 for their efforts "for their work for the peaceful termination of the apartheid regime, and for laying the foundations for a new democratic South Africa."

In 1994, Mandela was elected South Africa's president and initiated economic, housing, and education initiatives to improve the living standards of the country's black population. Mandela did not seek a second term as president but remained a strong international presence advocating for social justice, reconciliation, and peace.

Nelson Mandela was no troublemaker. He was one of the greatest peacemakers the world has ever known. Can you imagine all that he suffered in his efforts to overcome the evils of apartheid in his home country? I can't, but the world is better for it.

As you might guess, there are hundreds of well-known Nelson Mandela quotes. The one that really caught my eye is when he observed, "As I have said, the first thing is to be honest with yourself. You can never have an impact on society if you have not changed yourself . . . Great peacemakers are all people of integrity, of honesty, but humility." That's a very telling statement about what it takes to be a peacemaker, whether it is on a local, non-publicized level or the international stage.

Developing a Conciliatory Attitude

In a world full of conflict and divisiveness, there are numerous ways to be a peacemaker. Allow me to offer you a lengthy list of tips for how you can make your contribution to being at peace with others and helping the world we to be at peace with itself.

Commit. If you are going to be a peacemaker, you have to make a strong commitment to being in that role. A lukewarm commitment to any endeavor in life isn't going to be helpful or effective, much less when you are trying to bring peace to a broken world and running into great opposition.

Don't Ignore Conflict or Smooth It Over Without Actually Resolving the Issue. Sometimes, we seek peace by sticking our head in the sand about what's happening and moving too quickly to a false peace where the underlying issue was never dealt with. Square up with what the conflict is and don't seek resolution in a superficial, watered-down way.

Focus on Righting Wrongs. A true peacemaker is focused on trying to deal with injustice in the world. They do so knowing that their best effort may not lead to peace because of what another person or group might do to sabotage the process. Nevertheless, peacemakers focus on righting wrongs in the world so that peace rather than war might break out.

Sacrifice Your Personal Comfort. The cost of being a peacemaker is pretty high. You will frequently find that you had to get out of your comfort zone emotionally and physically by going where the conflict is and doing what you can to resolve it. Given that we are comfort-oriented creatures, that is not an easy thing to do.

Speak Words that Encourage and Build Up, Not Words That Discourage and Tear Down. The tongue is a powerful force and can be used for good or evil. Make sure the words that come out of our mouth are constructive, accurate, and well-intentioned, aimed at moving everyone in the direction of peace.

Use Your Time, Talents, and Treasures to Benefit Others. Being at peace with others means being willing to sacrifice your time, abilities, and financial resources. To be at peace with people, we have to be willing to do what it takes to leave them better off, even when it comes at our expense.

Listen with Humility and Patience. Far too often, we want to be listened to rather than listen. We want to be understood rather than understand. When trying to make peace, get in listening mode and be patient enough to let the other person help you understand where they are coming from and what it's going to take to achieve peace.

Approach Others with Compassion, Especially Those Who Lack Self-Awareness. Some people don't have much self-awareness when it comes to understanding themselves and what's going on inside of them. Be as compassionate as you can when you're dealing with someone whose view of themselves and the issue at hand is an inch deep and a mile wide.

Look for What You Did Wrong and Fix It. When you are at odds with someone, look for what you did to cause the rupture in the relationship and repair it. Ask yourself, "What did I do to play into this conflict?"

Check Your Motivations. If you are trying to be at peace with someone, make sure you are doing it for their sake and not just your own. In your efforts to repair things, make sure you are not trying to make yourself look good or prove yourself right. If you are trying to make peace with someone just to make yourself feel better, you aren't ready yet.

Acknowledge Human Worth and Dignity. Never lose sight of the fact that each person has inherent worth and dignity. Even if someone has wounded you deeply by doing something despicable, he or she still has worth and are to be treated with civility.

Engage Nonviolently. If you are going to engage with someone in an effort to be at peace, watch out for your tendency to be verbally and physically aggressive and abusive. Speak and act in kind and loving ways—that will give both more power.

Forgive Before You Talk. Don't try to be at peace with someone you haven't forgiven. If you haven't forgiven them yet, it will leak out during your peacemaking efforts and sabotage what you are trying to do.

Support Cultural Diversity and Individual Uniqueness. We come from a wide variety of backgrounds, races, and cultural contexts. Consequently, we do things differently. Be supportive of cultural diversity—ways people live their lives differently from you. At the same time, don't ever support cultural diversity if it involves a culture engaging in immorality.

The world we live in is full of conflict. I hope these tips for how to do your part to be a peacemaker were helpful. While there are a lot of good books on being a peacemaker, the one I most highly recommend is Ken Sande's book *The Peacemaker*. Written from a Christian perspective, it is an important book about how to be an effective peacemaker in a world full of strife and conflict.

Some Final Thoughts

Eleanor Roosevelt rightly observed, "It isn't enough to talk about peace. One must believe in it. And it isn't enough to believe in it. One must work at it." We can't just sit back and hope that peace with others around the globe will just show up on our doorstep. As we say here in Texas, we have to grab the bull by the horns and make it happen. In a world soaked in strife, we have to actively pursue peace everywhere we can.

"Blessed are the peacemakers, for they will be called children of God" (Matthew 5:9). Nelson Mandela must have been one blessed person given how much of a peacemaker he was. To be a peacemaker, one would do well to follow in his footsteps—humble, never ignored conflict or falsely tried to smooth it over, service-oriented, believed in the worth and dignity of people, committed to the cause of peace, courageous and unflinching in standing up to troublemakers, and fully aware that even the most purely motivated efforts to facilitate peace on the planet are going to run into stiff opposition.

Think About It

1. Where have you tended to be a troublemaker in life, stirring up conflict and dissension?

2. Where have you made efforts to resolve conflict with others and be at peace with them?

3. Where have you tried to help others experiencing conflict be at peace?

Chapter 24

Give, Give, Give, and Give Some More:
A Charitable Attitude

Not he who has much is rich, but he who gives much.

—Erich Fromm

Whoever is kind to the poor lends to the LORD, and he
will reward them for what they have done.

—Psalm 19:17

I'm proud of our country in so many ways. One of the things I'm proudest
of is the United States' charitable giving. Every year, the Charities Aid
Foundation (CAF) publishes its World Giving Index. Over the last ten
years, the United States has been *the most generous country* in the world.
That's fantastic, don't you think? Aren't you proud of that as an American?
The Bible says, "From everyone who has been given much, much will be
required" (Luke 12:48, NASB). I think God has given this country a great
deal, and it makes me proud that we have given so much back.

Having said all this, I want to switch our focus from how much charity
a country gives to other countries to the charity we need to give to those
we are closest to. English clergyman and historian Thomas Fuller famously
said, "Charity begins at home, but should not end there." Whether he meant
it this way or not, I'm going to interpret "home" in the most intimate of
ways, the loved ones we are the most involved with.

Doing as much counseling as I do, it is painful to see how uncharitable husbands and wives can be to each other, how uncharitable fathers and mothers can be to their children, how uncharitable kids can be to their parents, how uncharitable siblings can be toward each other, and how uncharitable friends can be to one another when it comes to giving their love.

With this in mind, let me tell you about my other best friend on the planet. From my point of view, he is one of the most charitable people I have ever known and has inspired me to go and do likewise. I know of very few people who give as much as he does, the kind of person that you sometimes have to encourage to think about himself more often. Still, he is a wonderful role model for us all.

The Bearer of Gifts, Great and Small

My buddy, Mark, is a veterinarian. From the time he was a young pup himself, he wanted to be a small animal vet. Like me in my efforts to get into graduate school to become a psychologist, Mark didn't immediately get into veterinary school out of college and had to work his fanny off to get accepted. He has been a veterinarian for over thirty years and has a great reputation among his clients and the other veterinarians in town.

If that is all you knew about Mark, you would have missed what I think is his most admirable attribute. Mark's a giver. I've known him for more than twenty-five years, and I have never seen anyone who gives as much of his time, talents, and treasures to others.

I first met Mark at church when he was teaching the young marrieds' class. Knowing that I love to teach and had a special place in my heart for young marrieds, he graciously invited me to teach the class with him and sacrificially allowed me to split the teaching responsibilities. That was just the start of how much he has given me over the years.

Mark and I developed a close friendship over time, and I got a much deeper look into how much he gives to people. Time and time again, he is always in give mode, meeting with people left and right, encouraging and comforting them as they went through difficult times. Mark's charitable attitude certainly extends to his own family in that he is always doing whatever he can to support and encourage them as they experience the ups and downs of life.

I have been on the receiving end of Mark's giving ways more times than I can count. The greatest gift he has ever given me is his friendship. He and I like a lot of the same things (music, sports, movies, current events) and have spent a ton of time enjoying these things together, building our friendship over the years.

While his friendship is the greatest gift he has ever given me, Mark is a gift-giver par excellence in other ways as well. Mark listens so carefully to the things you say that he frequently goes out and gets what you were talking about so that you can enjoy it. Let me give you an example.

Mark and I love music. There aren't many people who can beat me when it comes to music trivia, but Mark is one of them. I have to go super-deep into my mental musical vault to find something Mark doesn't know about. Sometimes, I will purposely learn something way off the radar grid regarding music trivia just to mock his music trivia knowledge and let him know who's the boss in this area of our relationship. Nevertheless, a zillion times over, he has out-triviaed me and brought up stuff I had never heard before. I must admit that there have been times when I thought Mark must have misspent his youth to know some of the musical stuff he knows, but that's a whole different matter.

The point I'm leading up to is that I have mentioned obscure songs I used to love growing up, and, the next time Mark and I got together, he would have tracked the song down and gotten me a copy of it for me. I'm talking here about hard to find stuff. That's a true friend. With the advent of Itunes and Spotify, Mark can't do that kind of thing anymore, so he has turned his attention to hunting down other things I wouldn't give to myself and given them to me. When someone pays that much attention to the things that mean a lot to you and goes to the effort and expense of trying to make sure you have them, that's a wonderful thing that strengthens and deepens a friendship.

Mark's taught me a lot about how to be a giver. He looks at people in such a way that no sacrifice of time, talents, or treasures is too much. He constantly has his ears perked up for how he can give to others and leave them better off. Mark gives and gives and gives, and, when his life is over, he will have spent it well.

Just like I used a previous chapter to hold my friend, Amir, up as a cheerful person, I hold my friend, Mark, up to you as a charitable person. Thanks, Mark, for giving me so much, more than I have ever given in return. Thanks for modeling for me what it looks like to constantly be in give mode rather than take mode. You have shown me, time and time again, what charity looks like.

Developing a Charitable Attitude

Some of you are already doing fine when it comes to giving to others. I would encourage you just to stay the course. For the rest of us, here are some tips for strengthening a charitable attitude toward others.

Pay Attention to What People Say They Need or Want. Good givers are good listeners. They hear things that the rest of us don't hear. Like a dog can hear a pitch that humans can't, givers can hear people express needs and wants in ways that don't get through to the rest of us. When you're interacting with others, try to listen with what we psychologists call the "third ear," the one that hears the things that go beyond the person's words. Try to make your interpersonal radar more sensitive for what people need or want that they can't or won't give to themselves and, within reason, give it to them.

Act on What You Heard. It's one thing to pick up on what someone says they need or want, a whole different thing to make sure you give it to them. Remember, the road to hell is paved with good intentions. Don't intend to give, give.

Give to Those Closest to You. Sometimes, we are so busy giving to the rest of the world that we neglect the people closest to us. Charity begins at home with loved one's by meeting their needs. If I am going to be charitable to my wife, children, grandchildren, and closest friends, I need to freely give them attention, acceptance, appreciation, affirmation, affection, comfort, encouragement, respect, support, and understanding. These psychological needs are pre-wired into the soul of every human being, and we are practicing charity of the highest kind when we meet these needs in others.

Give to Those You Don't Know. We live in a world full of needy people. I would encourage you to think outside the box about giving your time, talents, and treasures to others in your community, across the country, and around the world who you don't know personally. We need to have love and compassion for humankind, not withhold it just because we don't have a personal relationship with someone.

Let Others Give to You. I've brought this up before, but we need to allow others to give to us. I've been prone to get in the way of others giving to me because I don't feel worthy of them doing so. Please, don't do that. Let others receive the blessing of blessing you. Remind yourself of how good it feels when others let you give to them, and let them experience that good feeling as well by allowing them to give to you.

Confucius said, "Charity, like the sun, brightens every object on which it shines." In light of that, we want to be charitable to *everyone* we encounter, even if it just takes the form of meeting their psychological needs, so that we brighten every person we meet. In a world that seems to be full of takers, let's take up residence in the givers group and brighten things up.

Some Final Thoughts

We need to develop a charitable attitude toward the people with whom we are the most intimately involved. When it comes to how much we give to them, we need to give the most. I like the way Marvin J. Ashton put it when he said,

> Perhaps the greatest charity comes when we are kind to each other, when we don't judge or categorize someone else, when we simply give each other the benefit of the doubt or remain quiet. Charity is accepting someone's differences, weaknesses, and shortcomings; having patience with someone who has let us down; or resisting the impulse to become offended when someone doesn't handle something the way we might have hoped. Charity is refusing to take advantage of another's weakness and being willing to forgive someone who has hurt us. Charity is expecting the best of each other.

That's a pretty good description of the kind of charity that needs to begin at home.

But we also need to give to the world at large, to be charitable toward those who are hungry, sick, poor, and oppressed. Maya Angelou wisely observed, "I've learned that you shouldn't go through life with a catcher's mitt on both hands; you need to be able to throw something back." For lack of a better way to put it, being charitable is throwing something back as you go through life, not always being on the receiving end. St. Augustine said, "Find out how much God has given you and from it take what you need; the remainder is needed by others." We are to be charitable by looking at how much we have been blessed with and giving away what we don't need. Remember, on the day you die, you can't take it with you.

Charity doesn't really always have to do with how wealthy a person or a country happen to be. One of the countries that is always at the top of the

Charitable Giving Index is Myanmar, a country that is ranked fifty-first in per capita wealth. Myanmar gives as much from its heart as it does its pocketbook. First and foremost, be charitable from your heart toward those God puts in your path. Your pocketbook can always be opened up later.

I close with one final quote. Comedian Bob Hope said, "If you haven't got any charity in your heart, you have the worst kind of heart trouble." Let's all keep working on having charitable hearts so that we don't die of uncharitable heart disease.

Think About It

1. If every person were a country, where do you think you would fall in the world rankings when it comes to being charitable?

2. When you're being charitable, is it usually from your pocketbook or your heart?

3. How do you feel when others are charitable by meeting your financial needs? Your psychological needs?

Chapter 25

Have the Highest Thoughts:
A Consecrated Attitude

> Nurture your mind with great thoughts, for you
> will never go any higher than you think.
>
> —Benjamin Disraeli

> Finally, brothers and sisters, whatever is true, whatever is noble, what-
> ever is right, whatever is pure, whatever is lovely, whatever is admira-
> ble—if anything is excellent or praiseworthy—think about such things.
>
> —Philippians 4:8

I n the second half of this book, I've focused on the attitudes that are good
for us, like having a caring, courageous, or conscientious attitude. In this
chapter, I want to take us up to 30,000 feet and talk about the highest and
most important attitude we can have in life, a consecrated attitude.

Merriam-Webster defines *consecrated* as "dedicated to a sacred
purpose" and *sacred* as "worthy of religious veneration." When we think
about a consecrated attitude, we typically think about the world's great
religions and the people who founded them. Whatever our spiritual or
religious orientation, even if we don't believe in God, we often turn to the
person or group we believe to have the highest view of people, the meaning of life, how to reach our full potential, and, if a higher power exists,
the nature and character of God.

You'll get a lot of different lists thrown at you for the world's great religions. One website I came cross suggests that there are currently as many as eighteen world religions: Atheism/Agnosticism, Baha'i, Buddhism, Christianity, Confucianism, Druze, Gnosticism, Hinduism, Islam, Jainism, Judaism, Rastafarianism, Shinto, Sikhism, Zoroastrianism, Traditional African religions, African Diaspora religions, and Indigenous American religions. Not being a student of world religions, I didn't even recognize half the list and know very little about each of these religions except for one.

In this chapter, I'm going to talk about the worldview I'm familiar with, Christianity. For me, Christianity has the highest view when it comes to all the truly important matters of life. Here, I'm not talking about how Christians have sometimes so grossly perverted the teachings and application of Christianity over the years. I'm talking about the real deal—Christianity in its purest form. From my perspective, Christianity nails it when it comes to helping us have an accurate understanding of why we are here and how we are to spend our lives.

Before I go there, I want to address any concerns you might have that this book has been a long and manipulative bait-and-switch meant to evangelize you about Christianity. It's not. As I have done in the previous chapters, I'm simply going to take you into the life of a person who, to my way of thinking, personified the attitude under examination, whether it was a good one or a bad one.

In my sixty-seven years on the planet, I know of no other historical figure who better exemplifies a consecrated attitude, one "dedicated to a scared purpose," than the person I'm about to discuss. I hope you can go there with me. If you can't, I want you to know I understand. If you are willing, let's move forward in our discussion.

Consecrated or Crazy?

Jesus was born 6/5 BCE in Judea into a Jewish family. To say that he didn't have a very good start in life would be an understatement. The king of Judea, Herod, caught wind of his birth and that he was viewed by some as the future king of the Jews. To squelch the possibility of that coming true, Herod had all the children two years of age or under in Judea murdered so he could eliminate any threat to his throne. Jesus' parents, Mary and Joseph, took him to Egypt to save his life and only returned when Herod was dead and his throne had been handed over to one of his equally despotic and evil sons.

The record of Jesus' life suggests he had to grow and mature like any other boy. His maturity appeared to reach a pretty high level early on when, as a twelve-year-old, he ditched his parents after a Jewish feast in Jerusalem and they found him in the temple courts listening to and questioning the rabbis, the leading religious experts of Judaism. That he was twelve is significant because that was the last year before a boy became a full participant in the life of the Jewish synagogue. It says, "Everyone who heard him was amazed at his understanding and his answers" (Luke 2:47). It goes on to say, he "grew in wisdom and stature" (Luke 2:52).

The next time we see Jesus, he is a thirty-year-old man. He is no longer listening to and questioning the Jewish rabbis, he is teaching and being questioned by them. Jesus' fame spread throughout the land, and he ended up making claims that led to his execution. The claim that ultimately led to his murder is that he was God in human form (John 10:30).

Related to that seemingly outlandish claim, Jesus said he was "the way, the truth, and the life" and that no one could enter into what Christians call a "born again" relationship with God except through him (John 14:6). Those claims led the Jewish high priest to become so angry he tore his own clothes, polled the rest of the religious leaders about what to do with this lunatic, physically and emotionally abused him, and turned him over to the Roman authorities to be executed on a cross.

Let's step back from all this for a second. When we explored the bad attitudes, we talked about the *cocky* superstar golfer, the *condescending* sports reporter, the *conceited* music entrepreneur, and the *caustic* awards show host. When we explored the good attitudes, we have talked about the *committed* "hidden figures" of NASA, the *compassionate* abolitionist, the *conciliatory* South African freedom fighter, the *caring* founder of the American Red Cross, the *conscientious* special counsel, and the *courageous* bus rider. When it comes to who we are going to talk about as the best earthly example of someone with a *consecrated* attitude, I think we have to look at the world's greatest religious leaders. We have to look at the people whose attitude and mission were truly sacred and decide who had the highest and most sacred attitude of all.

Let me briefly lay out ten of the highest attitudes Jesus taught and practiced in life, further evidence to me that he has no equal among people. As you go through the list, ask yourself if you, anyone you know, or any of the greatest religious leaders taught and non-hypocritically practiced these principles.

- **Love your enemies** (Matthew 5:44). Jesus knew it was easy to love those who treat us well but incredibly hard to love those who treat us badly, a whole new shift in thinking.

- **Treat others like you want them to treat you** (Matthew 7:12). Jesus taught that what we call "the Golden Rule" properly summed up the Jewish law and what the prophets had taught throughout the centuries.

- **Forgive those who have hurt you** (Mark 11:25). Jesus understood that unforgiveness is "like drinking poison and hoping the other person would die." He knew forgiving others was one of the most important keys to a healthy life.

- **The first will be last, the exalted will be humbled** (Matthew 23:12). Jesus was a staunch opponent of pride and arrogance, knowing that all they do is precipitate our fall in life.

- **Live to serve, not to take** (Matthew 20:26–28). One of the major themes of the life of Jesus was the emphasis on serving others rather than have them serve you.

- **Turn the other cheek** (Matthew 5:38–39). Jesus taught that if someone insults you it is better to be insulted twice than to take someone to court. Turning the other cheek was not meant to encourage people to tolerate abuse or to never sue someone, it was meant to promote having a thicker skin and a warmer heart in our dealings with others.

- **You can't serve two masters** (Matthew 6:24). Jesus was wise enough to know that we can't serve two masters in life and that, if we try to, we end up being devoted to one and despising the other. Jesus challenged all his listeners to make up their minds as to who or what was going to be their central focus and devotion in life.

- **Don't worry about your circumstances** (Matthew 6:25–27). Jesus directed everyone back to God, not circumstances, for where to have peace and contentment in life. Specifically, he tried to get people to trust in the sovereignty of God (he's in control even if it doesn't seem so) and his goodness (God is out to help us, not to harm us).

- **Only a few find the way to true life** (Matthew 7:13–14). Jesus wasn't trying to be a downer here; he was simply stating the path to the abundant life is narrow and rarely traveled and that the gate to personal destruction is broad and frequently traveled.

- **Gain the world, forfeit your life** (Mark 8:34–37). Jesus repeatedly reminded us that the earth is not our true home, that we are sojourners while here, and that we need to look beyond the temporal pleasures of wealth, power, and sex to what is eternally valuable.

- **Give from your abundance to the poor** (Mark 10:21). Jesus didn't preach a life of unhealthy austerity, but he talked a lot about the fact that those of us who have a lot in life need to share with those who have very little. The "haves" need to give to the "have nots" in healthy and appropriate ways.

- **"Hate" your family** (Luke 14:25–27). Here, "hate" means to "love less." The principle expressed by Jesus here is that your love for God is to be so noticeably stronger than your love for people and things that it looks like you "hate" them by comparison.

These teachings were quite radical 2000 years ago when Jesus taught them. They still are, even among us post-modern types. Other world religions teach some of these things, but Jesus claimed that he was the *authoritative* source of these teachings and came to challenge humanity to adopt them. To my knowledge, no other world religion makes the claim that its founder is God in human form and has the authority to tell us how to live.

If Jesus really was God incarnate and "the way, the truth, and the life" (John 14:6), everything he taught is worthy of "religious veneration" and the highest of all the views offered to mankind. If he wasn't, Jesus was one of the biggest lunatics and narcissists who ever walked the planet and unworthy of our devotion. Where one lands on whether or not Jesus was divine is totally and completely up to each individual.

C. S. Lewis made the following observation about Jesus, "You must make your choice: either this man was, and is, the Son of God, or else a madman or something worse. You can shut him up for a fool, you can spit at him and kill him as a demon; or you can fall at his feet and call him Lord and God. But let us not come with any patronizing nonsense about his being a great human teacher. He has not left that open to us. He did not intend to." Jesus, unlike the leaders of all the greatest spiritual movements in human history, claimed to be more than merely human. As Lewis put it, Jesus didn't leave the option open to us of calling him a great teacher or even viewing him as the founder of one of the world's great religions.

Since you don't know me, you can't know if what I'm about to say is true or just me blowing smoke. But, let me say it anyway. Even if I hadn't become a Christian when I was young, I believe I still would have ended up believing that of all the people who have ever lived Jesus stands head and shoulders above the rest. During his thirty-three years on earth, Jesus turned everything upside down in how we view reality and how we are supposed to live our lives. There is no single human being who has had a greater positive impact on our world than him.

If you haven't already, I would ask you to strongly consider Jesus as the highest example of a consecrated attitude. Doesn't it make sense that some-one who taught to love your enemies was operating on a much higher plane than the rest of us? Doesn't it make sense that someone who talked about the importance of forgiveness rather than preaching "an eye for an eye" had loftier things figured out about life? Doesn't it make sense that someone talking about serving rather than being served and humbling rather than exalting yourself was operating at a more sacred and holy level than the rest of us?. Separate and apart from whether or not he was God in human form, who else would you want to aspire to be like?

If you aren't spiritually oriented, may I encourage to look at Jesus from the perspective of whether or not any other human being compares to him. If you do nothing but look at him that way, I think you will find Jesus to be the best earthly choice for who to model your life after and whose attitude to try to make your own. Do yourself a favor. Study how he lived his life, how he treated others, whether or not he practiced what he preached, whether or not he was a giver or a taker, and any other measure of assessing his depth and character as a human being that we might use. Do any others compare?

Near the end of his life, Napoleon Bonaparte came to the same con-clusion, saying, "I know men, and I tell you Jesus Christ was not a man. Superficial minds see a resemblance between Jesus and the founders of empires and the gods of other religions. That resemblance does not exist. There is between Christianity and other religions the distance of infinity." He was right about one thing and wrong about another. Bonaparte was right that Jesus Christ "was not a man" in the sense that any others could be compared to him. The world had never seen anyone like Jesus before he arrived, and it has never seen anyone like him since he left.

I think Bonaparte was wrong to say "Christianity and other religions" because Christianity is actually not a religion. Jesus didn't come to start a new religion; he came to implement a whole new way of looking at life and pursuing an intimate relationship with God. For Jesus, it was a radical "out with the old, in with the new."

Developing a Consecrated Attitude

To develop a consecrated attitude, we have to decide who had the most sacred mindset of all and understand the distinguishing factors of his or her view of reality. Given that I have offered you Jesus as the single highest example of someone with a consecrated attitude, let me give you some tips on what developing his attitude might involve.

Work on a "Others Must Increase and I Must Decrease" Attitude. A consecrated attitude is a humble attitude. Even if our thoughts are wiser than someone else's, we don't walk around with our chests puffed out acting like arrogant jerks. Even if we act in a more moral manner than others, we need to remember that all of us fall far short of the moral perfection of God. On our best day, we don't know .00000001% of all the things God knows and don't come anywhere close to being as morally pure and upright as he is. We need to avoid any hint of thinking more highly or ourselves than we ought.

Work on a "Service-Oriented" Attitude. A consecrated attitude is a service-oriented attitude. If we have a sacred sense of purpose in life, we spend each day trying to serve others, not manipulatively trying to get them to serve us. This doesn't mean we don't let others serve us, it just means we try to "beat them to the punch" and serve them before they can serve us. Our daily "homework" is to be on the lookout for what others need (physically, emotionally, and spiritually) and do the best we can to meet those needs.

Work On an "Other-Centered" Attitude. A consecrated attitude is a selfless attitude. Narcissists are constantly thinking about themselves—how awesome they are, that they are better than everyone else, and the like. Other-centeredness means that you drop your self-centered, egocentric way of looking at things at the door each day and focus more on other people's lives than you do your own.

Work on a "Don't Want or Need People's Approval" Attitude. A consecrated attitude leads you to feel indifferent to whether or not others like or approve of you. This isn't to say that you go out and purposely act badly to hurt people or tick them off. You make an internal decision to avoid "playing to the crowd" and express your *real self* whether people like you or agree with you. You remain true to your core values and let public opinion fall where it may. You never look at your popularity rating, only whether or not you are living a life of integrity.

Work on a "Willing to Pay the Price" Attitude. A consecrated attitude will put you in the line of fire with those who thoughts are low and shallow. If you have consecrated thoughts that you're willing to express and live by, you can expect to be attacked and persecuted for it. Malevolent, dark-minded people cannot tolerate a consecrated attitude, and they will do everything they can to silence those who have one. That's why Jesus was executed as a common criminal. His thoughts were so radically different and offensive to the non-consecrated thoughts of the religious and political leaders of the day that they felt they had no other choice but to "eliminate the opposition."

When the Bible says, "In your relationships with one another, have the same mindset as Jesus Christ: Who, being in very nature God, did not consider equality with God something to be used to his advantage; rather, he made himself nothing by taking the very nature of a servant, being made in human likeness" (Philippians 2:5–7), it's saying some incredibly important things about what the most consecrated attitude is—one of humility. We live in a day and age where humility is in short supply, and that is perhaps the major reason we treat each other so badly.

Some Final Thoughts

All this talk about a consecrated attitude reminds me of the movie *The Karate Kid*. The movie is about a fifteen-year-old kid, Daniel LaRusso, who moves with his mother from New Jersey to southern California and experiences the culture shock of his life. Daniel gets sideways with some of the "cool" guys in high school, and they beat him up and damage his bike using karate skills they learned from a cocky martial arts teacher in town. Mr. Miyagi, the maintenance man for the apartment complex Daniel lives in, takes Daniel under his wing teaches him karate.

Mr. Miyagi's methods for teaching Daniel karate are unorthodox to say the least (who can forget "Wax on, wax off"?). Daniel chafes at Mr. Miyagi's teaching methods until a pivotal moment where Mr. Miyagi helps Daniel to see that his methods are 500 miles ahead of Daniel's ability to grasp. Daniel finally humbles himself to Mr. Miyagi's tutelage and goes on to defeat the boys who beat him up in a regional karate championship.

Daniel's thoughts were not Mr. Miyagi's thoughts throughout most of the movie. There was very little overlap between how Daniel viewed reality and how Mr. Miyagi viewed it. As their relationship deepened, Daniel began to think more the way Mr. Miyagi thought and learned how to do things right in life. At a pivotal moment in the movie, Daniel "got it," hit his stride, and was able to learn karate at a high level.

I think there is a parallel to our lives when it comes to God. I think of God as Mr. Miyagi but on massive steroids. God tries everyday to help us see life from his very unusual and counter-intuitive perspective, and all most of us do is chafe at his teachings. God tries to give us the highest and most consecrated ways to view reality, and all most of us do is act like he can't rub two neurons together and throw his genius back in his face. The highest truth God gives us is that he exists, loves us, and wants to have a close relationship. Those who don't believe in God or believe he exists but is indifferent toward us, have, from a Chrisitan perspective, bought into the two worst attitudes a person can have in life and are truly lost.

I encourage you, as a fellow struggler whose attitude is just as broken and damaged as yours, to spend the rest of your life pursuing the highest thoughts, the ones that are true, noble, right, pure, lovely admirable, excellent, and praiseworthy. The bad attitudes we explored in the first half of the book are the ones that are untrue, ignoble, wrong, impure, ugly, unworthy, poor, and blameworthy. They are beneath our dignity as human beings and only cause ourselves and others around us great harm. The thoughts of God are the ones that will do us the most good and help our lives to soar as if on wings of eagles.

Think About It

1. As you look back at the bad attitudes we've covered, which two or three have you struggled with the most? How much damage have they caused your life?

2. As you look back at the good attitudes we've covered, which two or three are the ones you have lived by and how much good have they done your life?

3. Who do you turn to for developing the highest, most consecrated thoughts for how to live life? On what basis do you believe what he or she teaches?

How to Have a Good Attitude for Life

Chapter 26

The Long and Winding Road to Improving Your Attitude

If you can't fly then run, if you can't run then walk, if you can't walk then crawl, but whatever you do you have to keep moving forward.

—Martin Luther King, Jr.

Let us not become weary in doing good, for at the proper time we will reap a harvest.

—Galatians 6:9

W e live in a world that prefers instant gratification, quick fixes, and immediate results. When it comes to changing our attitude, wanting a fast turnaround in how we view reality will only discourage us and lead to throwing in the towel. Our attitude, the good, the bad, and the ugly, didn't get there overnight. Like it or not, we need to spend the rest of our lives working to hold on to our good attitudes and let go of our bad ones.

Even after reading this book, your bad attitudes are still firmly entrenched in your mind and will never totally go away. The best hope any of us can have is to atrophy these attitudes over time by accepting that we have them, be compassionate about the fact that they are keeping us from enjoying a richer and fuller life, and diligently move in the direction of internalizing good attitudes so that we can experience greater emotional, relational, and spiritual health.

Nothing of true value comes easily. This is especially true when it comes to moving away from all bad attitudes we have and going in the direction of the good ones. You've got to have two things to pull this off, courage and discipline. It takes courage to be willing to change your view of things, especially when you have thought a certain way for so long. And, it takes discipline to change your attitude because you have to "work out your mental salvation" each and every day. Courage and discipline are the foundation of any valid effort to improve your attitude and reclaim your life.

All of us have a realistic chance to go from bad attitudes to good ones. We have free will and can choose our attitude each day. Just because we have thought a certain way all our life doesn't mean we have to keep thinking that way. We can move in the direction of a good attitude no matter our age, skin color, gender, family of origin, life experiences, education level, or country of birth.

Changing our attitude for the better involves all three aspects of our soul: mind, emotions, and will. We can think our way to a better attitude, we can feel our way to a better attitude, and we can act our way to a better attitude.

The list that follows is my best effort to encourage you in all three ways. Pretty much everything I'm about to suggest falls into the "easier said than done" category, but don't let that become an excuse for not doing these things. I'm reminded of President Kennedy's speech about going to the moon, where he said, "We choose to go to the moon in this decade and do the other things, not because they are easy, but because they are hard." Choose to work on improving your attitude not because it is easy but because it is hard and will bring out courage and discipline inside of you that you didn't know you had.

Fifty Ways to Leave a Bad Attitude Behind

1. Accept (not like) that you have a bad attitude and that it has made your life more emotionally and relationally painful and dysfunctional. Don't try to argue with your bad attitude, suppress it, fix it, or make it go away. It is what it is. Accept it.

2. Accept the fact that while you're on the planet your broken/fallen mind works against you and is bent in the direction of the bad attitudes, not the good ones.

3. Read this book once a year (and, of course, get your friends to buy a copy).

4. Take your top two or three worst attitudes and write down the emotional, relational, physical, and spiritual cost of each.

5. Have compassion (empathy and sympathy) that you have these bad attitudes, that they have been costly, and that your mind is working against you.

6. Surround yourself with good attitudinal role models. Bad attitudinal company corrupts your attitude, good attitudinal company helps.

7. Write out the many ways your life will improve if you move in the direction of the good attitudes.

8. Decide who you are going to turn to for your highest, most consecrated beliefs about life.

9. Set aside time each day to meditate on the good attitudes.

10. Put your will in the direction of the good attitudes and act on them as if they are true (fake it til you make it).

11. Focus on the blessings of your life and express gratitude for them.

12. Use more accurate speech, avoiding words like *never, always, awful, horrible* and the like.

13. Try to not take yourself too seriously. Laugh a lot more.

14. Express gratitude to others for the kind things they do.

15. Forgive people for how they have wounded you.

16. Celebrate your victories, even the small ones.

17. Treat people in a civil manner, even people you can't stand.

18. Calm your mind down and be more aware of and curious about the thoughts and feelings you have each day.

19. Breathe.

20. View your thoughts and feelings from a distance and acknowledge that you are much more than what you think or feel.

21. Change what you can in life and try to turn the rest over to God.

22. Reframe your difficulties and struggles in life as a chance to grow and mature.

23. Enjoy nature.

24. Practice visual imagery by focusing on relaxing and calming images.

25. Exercise and get in shape.

26. Eat right.

27. Do the hard things first each day.

28. Be assertive and firmly address the things bothering you.

29. Give rather than take.

30. Apologize and make amends to people you've hurt.

31. Offer solutions and not criticisms or complaints to others.

32. Be quick to listen, slow to speak, and even slower to wrath.

33. Seek to understand, not to be understood.

34. Develop some healthy, appropriate "mantras" for yourself ("Live in the here and now," "Take a deep breath," "Be compassionate," "Accept reality," "To err is human," "You can't please everyone," "The virtue lies in the struggle, not the prize," "It is more blessed to give than to receive," "There's no gain without pain").

35. Work on having an accurate attitude rather than a positive or negative one.

36. Develop your talents and abilities so you keep getting better at things.

37. Figure out what your core values are and keeping moving in the direction of living your life according to them.

38. Have more empathy and compassion toward others given how difficult life is for all of us.

39. Work on self-control rather than controlling others.

40. Be thankful for what you have, even if it isn't as much as others have.

41. Look for the best in others while not ignoring their flaws.

42. Obey the rules, even the irritating, stupid, and unnecessary ones.

43. Acknowledge there is only one God and you ain't it.

44. See others as your equals regardless of their lot in life.

45. Only be confident you can pull something off if you have the ability to do it, have prepared, and have removed all the risks you can.

46. Have the courage to stand up and fight for what is right.

47. Be a good Samaritan by taking care of those in need.

48. Give of your time, talents, and treasures to help others.

49. Make peace with those who are willing to make peace with you.

50. Dedicate your thoughts to nobler and higher things.

I warned you that all of these things are easier said than done. But, can you imagine how much better your life would be if you got better at doing just a few of them? You wouldn't even recognize the old you! Others wouldn't recognize the old you either!

Some Final Thoughts

We have come a long way together. Thank you for traveling alongside me as we explored how important attitude is, what the worst ones are, what the best ones are, and the different ways we can improve our attitude over time.

I want to challenge you, as someone whose attitude is as bad as yours, to keep working on improving your attitude as you go through life. Don't grow weary of working on this incredibly important issue. Benjamin Disraeli was spot on when he said, "Nurture your mind with great thoughts, for you will never go any higher than you think." While we can't control the trials and tribulations that come our way in life, we can work on having the right attitude about them and how we respond to them.

The Apostle Paul said, "When I was a child, I talked like a child, I thought like a child, I reasoned like a child. When I became a man, I put the ways of childhood behind me" (1 Corinthians 13:11). The twelve bad attitudes we covered are the ways we thought when we were children. Sadly, too many of us have brought these childish and destructive attitudes with us into adulthood. The twelve good attitudes we explored are the ways we need to think if we are going to become full-fledged adults.

I've thrown hundreds of quotes at you throughout this book. In closing, I'm going to end with one I used in chapter 1, the quote by Viktor Frankl that came out of his experiences in Nazi death camps. I would encourage you to memorize it and repeat it to yourself each day.

> We who lived in concentration camps can remember the men who walked through the huts comforting others, giving away their last piece of bread. They may have been few in number, but they offer sufficient proof that everything can be taken from a man but one thing: the last of the human freedoms—*to choose one's attitude in any given set of circumstances*, to choose one's own way.

The freedom we have to choose our attitude is the greatest of all our freedoms. Viktor Frankl knew this powerful truth when he was interred in Nazi concentration camps. He understood that evil forces could take everything from him but his attitude, and he made a conscious choice to have the best attitude he could in an effort to survive the horrible things he experienced. Each of us have that same option available to us, to choose our attitude regardless of the situation we are in.

Choose your attitude wisely, my friend. Your attitude, not your circumstances, is what makes or breaks you as you go through life. I'll be praying for you. Pray for me.

Secular Attitude Quotes

- Thomas Jefferson: "Nothing can stop the man with the right mental attitude from achieving his goal; nothing on earth can help the man with the wrong mental attitude."
- Anne Brashares: "Your problem isn't the problem, it's your attitude about the problem."
- William James: "The greatest revolution of our generation is the discovery that human beings, by changing the inner attitudes of their minds, can change the outer aspects of their lives."
- Oprah Winfrey: "The greatest discovery of all time is that a person can change his future by merely changing his attitude."
- John Maxwell: "The greatest day in your life and mine is when we take total responsibility for our attitudes. That's the day we truly grow up."
- Maya Angelou: "If you don't like something, change it. If you can't change it, change your attitude."
- Irving Berlin: "Our attitudes control our lives. Attitudes are a secret power working twenty-four hours a day, for good or bad. It is of paramount importance that we know how to harness and control this great force.
- Anne Frank: "I don't think of all the misery but of the beauty that still remains."
- Chuck Swindoll: "We cannot change our past. We cannot change the fact that people act in a certain way. We cannot change the inevitable. The only thing we can do is play on the one string we have, and that is our attitude."

- Amy Tan: "If you can't change your fate, change your attitude."

- Albert Einstein: "Weakness of attitude becomes weakness of character."

- Louise Hay: "Everything in your life, every experience, every relationship is a mirror of the mental pattern that is going on inside of you."

- M. Scott Peck: "The quickest way to change your attitude toward pain is to accept the fact that everything that happens to us has been designed for our spiritual growth."

- Katherine Mansfield: "Could we change our attitude, we should not only see life differently, but life itself would come to be different."

- Earl Nightingale: "A great attitude does much more than turn on the lights in our worlds; it seems to magically connect us to all sorts of serendipitous opportunities that were somehow absent before the change."

- Sue Patton Thoele: "Abundance is, in large part, an attitude."

- Viktor Frankl: "We who lived in concentration camps can remember the men who walked through the huts comforting others, giving away their last piece of bread. They may have been few in number, but they offer sufficient proof that everything can be taken from a man but one thing: the last of the human freedoms—to choose one's attitude in any given set of circumstances, to choose one's own way."

- Helen Keller: "Everything has its wonders, even darkness and silence, and I learn, whatever state I may be in, therein to be content."

- Benjamin Disraeli: "Nurture your mind with great thoughts, for you will never go any higher than you think."

- John Maxwell: "People may hear your words, but they feel your attitude."

- Lou Holtz: "Ability is what you're capable of doing. Motivation determines what you do. Attitude determines how well you do it."

- Norman Vincent Peale: "Change your thoughts and you change your world."

- Michael Jordan: "My attitude is that if you push me towards something that you think is a weakness, then I will turn that perceived weakness into a strength."

- Andy Gilbert: "It's not the method, it's the mindset."
- Scott Hamilton: "The only disability in life is a bad attitude."
- Norman Vincent Peale: "Any fact facing us is not as important as our attitude toward it, for that determines our success or failure."
- David Steindl-Rast: "Any change in attitude changes the way one sees the world, and this in turn changes the way one acts."
- Wilferd Peterson: "Be gentle with yourself, learn to love yourself, to forgive yourself, for only as we have the right attitude toward ourselves can we have the right attitude toward others."
- Antoine de Saint-Exupery: "The meaning of things lies not in the things themselves, but in our attitude towards them."
- Leo Buscaglia: "There are two big forces at work, external and internal. We have very little control over external forces such as tornadoes, earthquakes, floods, disasters, illness and pain. What really matters is the internal force. How do I respond to those disasters? Over that I have complete control."
- Tom Stoppard: "A healthy attitude is contagious but don't wait to catch it from others. Be a carrier."
- Martin Luther King, Jr.: "Forgiveness is not an occasional act, it is a constant attitude."
- Dale Carnegie: "Take charge of your attitude. Don't let someone else choose it for you."
- Robert Foster Bennett: "Spend some time this weekend on home improvement; improve your attitude toward your family."
- Mark A. Brennan: "Attitude will always define who we are in life."
- Bob Proctor: "Gratitude is an attitude that hooks us up to our source of supply. And the more grateful you are, the closer you become to your maker, to the architect of the universe, to the spiritual core of your being. It's a phenomenal lesson."
- Colin Powell: "Excellence is not an exception, it is a prevailing attitude."
- Ralph Waldo Emerson: "To different minds, the same world is a hell, and a heaven."

Sacred Attitude Quotes

Philippians 4:8: "Finally, brothers and sisters, whatever is true, whatever is noble, whatever is right, whatever is pure, whatever is lovely, whatever is admirable—if anything is excellent or praiseworthy—think about such things."

Philippians 2:1–2: Therefore if you have any encouragement from being united with Christ, if any comfort from his love, if any common sharing in the Spirit, if any tenderness and compassion, then make my joy complete by being like-minded, having the same love, being one in spirit and of one mind."

Romans 8:6: "The mind governed by the flesh is death, but the mind governed by the Spirit is life and peace."

Mark 12:30: "Love the Lord your God with all your heart and with all your soul and with all your mind and with all your strength."

Romans 12:2: "Do not conform to the pattern of this world, but be transformed by the renewing of your mind. Then you will be able to test and approve what God's will is—his good, pleasing and perfect will."

Ephesians 4:22: "You were taught, with regard to your former way of life, to put off your old self, which is being corrupted by its deceitful desires; to be made new in the attitude of your minds."

Romans 15:5–6: "May the God who gives endurance and encouragement give you the same attitude of mind toward each other that Christ Jesus had, so that with one mind and one voice you may glorify the God and Father of our Lord Jesus Christ."

Romans 8:5: "Those who live according to the flesh have their minds set on what the flesh desires; but those who live in accordance with the Spirit have their minds set on what the Spirit desires."

Isaiah 55:9: "As the heavens are higher than the earth, so are my ways higher than your ways and my thoughts than your thoughts."

Psalm 92:5: "How great are your works, Lord, how profound your thoughts!"

Psalm 139:17: "How precious to me are your thoughts, God! How vast is the sum of them!"

Psalm 139:23: "Search me, God, and know my heart; test me and know my anxious thoughts."

Romans 12:3: "For by the grace given me I say to every one of you: Do not think of yourself more highly than you ought, but rather think of yourself with sober judgment, in accordance with the faith God has distributed to each of you."

Suggested Readings

Addiction

Addiction and Grace, by Gerald May

Addictions: A Banquet in the Grave, by Ed Welch

Anger

The Anger Workbook, by Les Carter and Frank Minirth

Anxiety/Worry

Calm My Anxious Heart, by Linda Dillow

The Anxiety Cure, by Archibald Hart

The Worry Workbook, by Les Carter and Frank Minirth

Balance

In Search of Balance, by Richard Swenson

Margin, by Richard Swenson

Bonding/Attachments

Hold Me Tight, by Sue Johnson

How We Love, by Milan and Kay Yerkovich

Wired for Love, by Stan Tatkin

Boundaries/Peacemaking

Boundaries, by Henry Cloud and John Townsend

The Peacemaker, by Ken Sande

Depression

Happiness is a Choice, by Frank Minirth and Paul Meier

The Depression Cure, by Stephen Ilardi

The Mindful Way Through Depression, by Mark Williams, John Teasdale, Zindel Segal, and Jon Kabat-Zinn

Emotional/Spiritual Health

Changes that Heal, by Henry Cloud

Emotionally Healthy Spirituality, by Peter Scazzero

Renovation of the Heart, by Dallas Willard

The Divine Conspiracy, by Dallas Willard

The Road Less Traveled, by M. Scott Peck

Forgiveness

Five Steps to Forgiveness, by Everett Worthington

The Art of Forgiving, by Lewis Smedes

Total Forgiveness, by R. T. Kendall

God

Knowing God, by J. I. Packer

Knowledge of the Holy, by A. W. Tozer

Grace

Grace Awakening, by Charles Swindoll

What's So Amazing about Grace?, by Philip Yancey

Marriage

Boundaries in Marriage, by Henry Cloud and John Townsend

Hope for the Separated, by Gary Chapman

Sacred Marriage, by Gary Thomas

Saving Your Marriage Before It Starts, by Les and Leslie Parrott

The Five Love Languages, by Gary Chapman

The Lies Couples Believe, by Chris Thurman

The Meaning of Marriage, by Tim and Kathy Keller

The Mystery of Marriage, by Mike Mason

Men's Issues

I Don't Want to Talk about It, by Terence Real

Men in Mid-Life Crisis, by Jim Conway

Men's Secret Wars, by Patrick Means

Point Man, by Steve Farrar

The Man in the Mirror, by Patrick Worley

When Men Think Private Thoughts, by Gordon MacDonald

Wild at Heart, by John Eldredge

Mindfulness

10% Happier: How I Tamed the Voice in My Head, Reduced Stress Without Losing My Edge and Found Self-Help that Actually Works—A True Story, by Dan Harris

Mindfulness: An Eight-Week Plan for Finding Peace in a Frantic World, by Mark Williams and Danny Penman

Mindfulness and Christian Spirituality: Making Space for God, by Tim Stead

Mindsight: The New Science of Personal Transformation, by Daniel Siegel

Right Here Right Now: The Practice of Christian Mindfulness, by Amy Oden

The Untethered Soul: The Journey Beyond Yourself, by Michael A. Singer

Wherever You Go There You Are: Mindfulness Meditation in Everyday Life, by Jon Kabat-Zinn

Personality Disorders

Freeing Yourself from the Narcissists in Your Life, by Linda Martinez-Lewi

Stop Walking on Eggshells, by Paul Mason and Randi Kreger

The Sociopath Next Door, by Martha Stout

Why Is It Always About You?, by Sandy Hotchkiss

Renewing Your Mind

Feeling Good, by David Burns

Get Out of Your Head, by Jennie Allen

Get Out of Your Mind and Into Your Life, by Stephen Hayes

Mind Over Mood, by Dennis Greenberger and Christine Padesky

Telling Yourself the Truth, by William Backus and Marie Chapian

The Lies We Believe, by Chris Thurman

The Lies We Believe About God, by Chris Thurman

Self-Compassion

Self-Compassion: Stop Beating Yourself Up and Leave Insecurity Behind, by Kristin Neff

The Mindful Self-Compassion Book: A Proven Way to Accept Yourself, Build Inner Strength, and Thrive, by Kristin Neff and Christopher Germer

The Self-Compassion Skills Workbook: A 14-Day Plan to Transform Your Relationship with Yourself, by Tim Desmond

Shame

Healing the Shame that Binds You, by John Bradshaw

I Thought It Was Just Me, by Brene Brown

Shame Interrupted, by Ed Welch

The Gifts of Imperfection, by Brene Brown

The Soul of Shame, by Curt Thompson

Suffering

Disappointment with God, by Philip Yancey

Where is God When it Hurts?, by Philip Yancey

Women's Issues

Breaking Free, by Beth Moore

Ever After, by Vicki Courtney

Finding Peace for Your Heart, by Stormie Omartian

Healing the Soul of a Woman, by Joyce Meyer

Lord, I Want to be Whole, by Stormie Omartian

Rest Assured, by Vicki Courtney

So Long, Insecurity, by Beth Moore

Worth

The Search for Significance, by Robert McGee

About the Author

C hris Thurman, PhD, is a psychologist, public speaker, and the author of numerous books, including the bestselling *The Lies We Believe*. He has spent his professional life writing and speaking about the destructive impact of faulty thinking on emotional, relational, and spiritual health. Chris and his wife, Holly, have been married for forty years, have three grown children who hung the moon, and three grandchildren who hung the moon even higher. In his leisure, Chris loves to hit golf balls into water hazards and is a devoted Texas Longhorn fan. Chris can be contacted at drchristhurman.com if you are interested in having him speak to your church or company.

www.ingramcontent.com/pod-product-compliance
Lightning Source LLC
Chambersburg PA
CBHW030307100426
42812CB00002B/595